6/25/19

FOLKLORE IN BALTIC HISTORY

FOLKLORE IN BALTIC HISTORY

RESISTANCE AND RESURGENCE

SADHANA NAITHANI

UNIVERSITY PRESS OF MISSISSIPPI / JACKSON

The University Press of Mississippi is the scholarly publishing agency of
the Mississippi Institutions of Higher Learning: Alcorn State University,
Delta State University, Jackson State University, Mississippi State University,
Mississippi University for Women, Mississippi Valley State University,
University of Mississippi, and University of Southern Mississippi.

www.upress.state.ms.us

The University Press of Mississippi is a member
of the Association of University Presses.

Library of Congress Cataloging-in-Publication Data

Names: Naithani, Sadhana, author.
Title: Folklore in Baltic history: resistance and resurgence / Sadhana Naithani.
Description: Jackson: University Press of Mississippi, [2019] | Includes
bibliographical references and index. |
Identifiers: LCCN 2018054048 (print) | LCCN 2018058048 (ebook) | ISBN
9781496823588 (epub single) | ISBN 9781496823595 (epub institutional) |
ISBN 9781496823601 (pdf single) | ISBN 9781496823618 (pdf institutional) |
ISBN 9781496823564 (cloth) | ISBN 9781496823571 (pbk.)
Subjects: LCSH: Baltic States—Folklore—History and criticism. | Folk
literature, Baltic—History and criticism. | Baltic States—Politics and
government—1940–1991. | LCGFT: Informational works.
Classification: LCC GR204 (ebook) | LCC GR204 .N34 2019 (print) | DDC
398.209479—dc23
LC record available at https://lccn.loc.gov/2018054048

British Library Cataloging-in-Publication Data available

CONTENTS

Preface   vii

Acknowledgments   ix

ONE   Writing a Dramatic History of Baltic Folkloristics:
Methodological Plurality and Multidisciplinarity   3

TWO   A Flashback   13

THREE   The Drama Begins   23

FOUR   Resistance Site 1: Folklore at the University   35

FIVE   Resistance Site 2: The Folklore Archives   43

SIX   Resistance Site 3: The Countryside   59

SEVEN   The Resurgence   89

Conclusion   101

References and Conversations   105

Index   111

PREFACE

This book should be seen as a nuanced representation of the relationship between folklore studies and a socialist-totalitarian state, based on some of the significant issues in the history of folklore studies in the three countries of Estonia, Latvia, and Lithuania, often referred to as "the Baltic countries." This is not a complete and comprehensive history of folkloristics in the Baltic countries, nor is it an even representation of all.

The central concern of this book is the international history of the discipline of folkloristics, which lets us see how varied, rich, and complex is the study of folklore across the globe. Ironically, the subject of study—folklore—is perceived as "simple," which implies that its study too is uncomplicated. The study of this "simple" subject is for a *variety* of reasons extremely complex and complicated. The "variety of reasons" are located in the many specific contexts in which folklore is studied. The universal application and acceptance of the concept often hide the temporal and spatial differences in its study. The dialectics of universality and particularity defines what connects folklorists across the world. This connection is rather unlike any other discipline because the universality of the concept lets them relate particularities across distances.

As a discipline, folklore studies has never been at the center of humanities, but its relationship to different political ideologies and political-ideological power structures has revealed its unique position within academia. Folkloristics is a discipline that creates a cusp between academic and popular politics. The fact that the name of its subject of study—folklore—implies a connection with the vast majority of nonruling sections and their perceptions about life and culture lends it a political-historical importance that overshadows the aesthetic power and pervasiveness of the folklore of any people. Within the Baltic countries, folklore studies have had an important place within and outside academia since the beginning of the twentieth century. Therefore, it is a significant location to study the relations of folkloristics with nationalism, socialism, and postsocialism. The subject of this book is folkloristics in Estonia, Latvia, and Lithuania during and after the regime of the USSR from 1944 to 1991.

ACKNOWLEDGMENTS

Research for this book was made possible by Spectress Project between Jawaharlal Nehru University, New Delhi, University of Tartu, Tartu, and University of Dublin, Dublin, and by the Partnership Development Grant 890-2013-17 from Canada's Social Science and Humanities Research Council. I am grateful to Professor Aditya Mukherjee and Dr. Ene Kõresaar for inviting me to the Department of Ethnology at the University of Tartu in 2016 and 2017 to pursue this research on the history of folkloristics in Estonia.

From Tartu, I traveled to Riga, Latvia, and to Vilnius, Lithuania, to research in the closely related historical processes in the three Baltic countries of Estonia, Latvia, and Lithuania. In all the three centers of folklore studies in the Baltic countries, my research was aided and encouraged by many scholars, and I am thankful to them all, not only for their help but also for their warmth and friendship.

In Tartu, Ülo Valk, Ene Kõresaar, Tiiu Jaago, Aigi Rahi-Tamm, Ergo Västrik, Kristin Kuutma, and Risto Järv shared their knowledge and experiences of research with me. I am extremely grateful for their intellectual generosity. For additional support in research—from administrative matters to scanning of books—Reet Russmann and Liilia Lannemann were always there, and I thank them for everything. I am especially thankful to Reet Russmann for organizing a tour of the countryside of southern Estonia as I wished to see the remnants of the Soviet period. I also thank Elo-Hanna Seljamaa and Merili Metsvahi, senior research fellows in the Department of Estonian and Comparative Folklore, for sharing their thoughts with me.

In Riga, Rita Treija, Toms Ķencis, and Baiba Krogzeme-Mosgorda were the people I first met with in the Archives of Latvian

Folklore in 2016. They introduced the archives, its collections, and its infrastructure to me, shared their knowledge with me, and connected me with other colleagues in 2016 and 2017. During my second visit, I also met and conversed with Aldis Pūtelis, Guntis Pakalns, Dace Bula, Beatrise Reidzāne, Māra Vīksna, and Ieva Garda Rozenberga (a former researcher in the Oral History Archives who accompanied me to the Latvian National Oral History Archives and organized a meeting with Māra Zirnīte, Edmunds Šūpulis, and Baiba Bela.). They shared with me their knowledge about research-ing and recording life stories in Latvia; this knowledge is not avail-able in English-language publications. The enthusiasm of each of these scholars for their research was inspiring, and their warmth was touching. I remain thankful to them. In Vilnius, Lina Būgienė helped me to understand many aspects of folklore scholarship and life under the Soviet rule in Lithuania. I am thankful to her for sharing personal experiences and research materials with me both during and after my visit. I am also thankful to her colleagues in the Folklore Archives and to Lina Leparskinė, Asta Skujytė, and Vita Džekčioriūtė-Medeišienė.

My long research stays in Tartu were made pleasant by Pihla Siim, Margaret Lyngdoh, Donee Lepcha, Ele Sepp, Tina Sepp and Maarja Valk. To them, I owe very warm thanks.

The experience of a research that combines empirical and theo-retical leaves the researcher with more than that which is expressed in the analytical work born of it. Research on Baltic folkloristics left me believing that the humility of Estonian, Latvian, and Lithuanian scholars is overwhelming: quietly working, never showing off their achievements, and probably genuinely feeling that they are "small" as nations and as populace. When I started with my research on the disciplinary history of folkloristics in Estonia, Latvia, and Lith-uania, I was met with the response, "Oh, really! But why?" When I said that I had the feeling that that "the present" of folkloristics was unfolding in the Baltics, the response was, "You think so?" As they started sharing with me recent publications, their plans in action, and their archives, it was my turn to say, "Oh, really? Amazing!" I am indeed grateful to all the people mentioned and to many others who enriched my experience of research.

FOLKLORE IN BALTIC HISTORY

CHAPTER ONE

WRITING A DRAMATIC HISTORY OF BALTIC FOLKLORISTICS

Methodological Plurality and Multidisciplinarity

This chapter provides an introduction to how this research on folkloristics in Estonia, Latvia, and Lithuania was conducted and how it has been conceptualized. The peculiarity of the situation lay in the researcher's incapability in the local languages, which was partly redeemed by substantial numbers of contemporary works by Baltic scholars in English language. Beyond that, it required new methods in accessing existing knowledge. The subject of folklore studies was entwined with history, politics, and ideology to such an extent that it could only be understood through a multidisciplinary approach. Every research situation is unique, but few have as many twists and turns as this one.

Why "Dramatic"?

In the twentieth century, the Baltic countries went through several major historical changes: they gained independence for the first time in modern history in 1918, were forced to accept Russian military presence in 1938/39, were occupied by Germany in 1941–1943, were occupied by the USSR in 1944, and gained freedom again in

1991. Three of these historical changes—in 1918, 1944, and 1991—impacted folklore in very different but definite ways. Each impact was dramatic in the way it happened, the radical changes it brought forth, and the intensity of participation by folklorists. The focus of this book is on the period from 1944 to the present, and the period between 1918 and 1944 is briefly explained.

The period from 1944 experienced many changes in quick succession to which scholars and institutions needed to adjust. The *Oxford English Dictionary* defines a dramatic event as one that is "sudden and striking." I call the period in Baltic folkloristics from 1944 to 1991 dramatic because it was full of not one but several sudden and striking changes. The nature of these events was such that they could be the stuff of which shocking stories are made. Accordingly, folklore research and teaching underwent dramatic changes. In the course of these dramatic circumstances, folklore researchers, collectors, and teachers—in short, folklorists—have done their work. For some of them, their personal lives were impacted in extreme ways.

What is Baltic folkloristics? one may ask. In spite of shared history and similarity of national destinies of Estonia, Latvia, and Lithuania, it is not very apt to speak of "Baltic" in the singular. Factually, there is no such thing as Baltic folkloristics in the sense of one reality or a single entity. Folkloristics in Estonia, Latvia, and Lithuania is differentiated not only by languages, but by many other specific details. Yet, this book attempts to discuss the folklore studies in the three countries simultaneously. The differences are neither considered insignificant nor ignored, because the differences and similarities together make the picture of Baltic folkloristics complete. The orientation of this work is tilted more toward comparable similarities. The reason for this approach is that similarities are far too many: the three countries were under the Soviet rule for exactly the same length of time; even before the Soviet rule, they had gained independence from their common and different foreign rulers around the same time—in 1918; they also freed themselves of the Soviet control at the same time—in 1991; and, finally, they themselves recognize their shared histories and are currently building collaborative networks for research and study of folklore. Similarities in folkloristics are in the ideological trajectory. Be it the early nationalist folklorists of the late nineteenth and early twentieth centuries, the folklorists under the Soviet rule, or those since independence from Soviet rule, the broad movement occurs along parallel lines. Within a span of some seventy years, folkloristics in the Baltics has experienced three major shifts. The changes in political history brought ideological shifts, and each shift caused a break from the past, creation of new structures, and generation of a different hope with the future.

Within the international history of the discipline, these and other ideological changes have been experienced elsewhere too. In any national context, the major concerns of the nation at any point of time have impacted the way folklore is studied, but the relationship may not always have been so close with the state power. Since the end of the Second World War in Western Europe and the simultaneous end of colonialism in Asia, folklore studies have been able to chart their course without being determined by the state directly. For example, the ideological shifts like feminist scholarship or postcolonial perspectives have been tangentially connected to social and political situations but have not been controlled/engineered by the state, nor have they necessarily changed the nature of the state. More often than not, the ideological shifts have remained matters of shifts in the academic paradigm without causing extreme changes in the institutions and individuals connected with folklore. In the Baltics, however, these shifts have meant changes in the lives of the folklorists, their institutions, and above all, in the life of the "folk" themselves. I find the changes to be dramatic in their scale and magnitude.

It is important to write about what happened to the discipline of folkloristics between 1944 and 1991 and what has been happening since then in the Baltic countries. It is important not only because it is part of the international history of the discipline of folkloristics, but also because its *specific* trajectory is a specific form of engagement of folklorists with the discipline. To this form of engagement belongs a specific sense of history: commitment to the discipline and resilience.

These *specific* aspects allow us to view and analyze more dimensions of the relationship between folkloristics, folklorists, and the powers that may be. The nature of this relationship in colonial contexts of Asia, Africa, and Latin America or in the nationalist contexts of Europe in nineteenth and twentieth centuries is known to the international community of folklore scholars. The relationships of folkloristics and folklorists to other kinds of power structures, like those of gender relations, have also been widely discussed. Marxism has exerted one of the important philosophical influences on these discussions. In contrast, we know relatively little about folkloristics and folklorists in the so-called socialist states and what Marxism has meant as the state ideology. In other words, the relationship between folklore and socialist powers has not been sufficiently grasped. This is not surprising because the socialist states have been, and the remaining ones continue to be, almost closed to researchers from the democratic world and presumably restrict their own scholars to freely share their research. The result is that we know very little about folkloristics in the states claiming to be followers of Marxism. In other words, our understanding of the relationship between Marxism and folklore remains theoretical. A study of the folkloristics in the Baltic countries from 1944 to 1991 allows us to see and analyze the praxis of folkloristics under a socialist regime.

The case of Baltic folkloristics under the socialist regime becomes even more interesting because it is preceded by a nationalism that was rightful in its assertion as the societies concerned had emerged from centuries-long colonial rules. Folklore had enjoyed a special status during this time (1918–1938). Then came the socialist rule as defined by the USSR, and after that came independence from the socialist rule. It is noteworthy that in the Baltic countries, folklore continued to remain academically and politically important during the Soviet period. This is what makes Baltic folkloristics one of the most complex and, simultaneously, significant fields in understanding the relationship between the discipline and the state. There may not be a similar field. The hegemonic power structures of academia do not let us easily see this and keep our attention focused on locations that are otherwise also more dominant on the international level. "Baltic folkloristics" is certainly not on the top of the charts of subjects in recent academic conferences, and few scholars even know what is going on here.

In this book, I am analyzing the development of folkloristics in the Baltic countries since their occupation by the USSR in 1944 and up to the present. One problem was studying a phase, like the Soviet period, that was so recent that supporting documents could not be found in the archives and that it has not yet been theorized upon by the Baltic folklorists themselves, at least not extensively, and definitely in hugely varying degrees in Lithuania, Latvia, and Estonia. Another problem was that the matters of the Soviet period are shrouded in mystery due to the nature of the Soviet system itself. Finally, and perhaps above all, was the problem of the researcher herself: I had little knowledge of Baltic history and know none of the Baltic languages, making my undertaking doubly difficult. However, I have endeavored to understand and present my understanding of Baltic folkloristics.

Methodological Plurality

My research is based on reading in two European languages—German and English—which meant that I could access the early folklore collections and writings, like those of Jakob Hurt and Oskar Loorits, which were in German. With English, I could access the research works produced by Baltic folklorists, ethnologists, and historians since 1991, which are increasingly in the English language.

However, I did not believe this to be enough to build my own understanding. I had more questions than could be answered by published research. So I decided to combine the readings with conversations with scholars, archivists, and researchers.

The conversations are an important aspect of my research methodology. They are not "interviews," but conversations; that is, there were no Q&A sessions. Needless to say, while an interview can be done with a consenting party, a conversation requires some amount of familiarity between the conversing parties. This familiarity between me and the Baltic scholars was based on different premises in each case. There were people I knew for years as fellow folklorists and friends, there were those that I got know in the process of this research, and there were those who attended my lectures on colonialism and folkloristics in 2008 when I was briefly visiting professor in the Tartu University and are today postdoctorate researchers and faculty members. I was to meet with all these people and record conversations with them during which we exchanged and shared information, opinions, experiences, and analyses. Initially, I thought of meeting with folklorists and folklore archivists, but as my research grew, I also met with ethnologists and historians. I met with senior scholars, some of who had been in the academic institutions as students or faculty during the Soviet period and with young researchers who have recently completed their PhDs. These conversations were planned and recorded on video. In most of the cases I had also read works by the scholars I was going to converse with. Readings and conversations got increasingly inter-linked as conversations were initiated on the basis of readings, but led to further readings being suggested by the scholars.

Multidisciplinarity

My analysis of Baltic folkloristics since 1944 emerges not only from readings and conversations about the history of folkloristics. In order to be able to understand this in the wider historical context, history books were available. As a folklorist, however, I wanted to understand the historical context with reference to the life of the "folk," that is, the common people, the nonruling sections of the populace. This search took me to the life stories of men and women who had experienced the Soviet time. "Life stories" clearly implies the story about the life lived, but hidden in its implication is the fact that life stories are narrated by the person whose story it is. It is thus a first-person narration and narrative. The methods of recording life stories were different in Latvia and in Estonia. In Latvia, the life stories were recorded on audio tapes by the National Oral History Archives. In Estonia, life stories as first-person narratives were written after the fall of the Soviet Union in 1989 as response to calls by the Cultural History Archives of the Estonian Literary Museum in the same year and again in later years.

> The Cultural History Archive of the Estonian Literature Museum published its first call for the collection of Estonian life-stories in the newspapers in the fall of 1989. The initiative derived largely from a young journalist Anneli Sihvart, who came to Rutt Hinrikus, former director of the manuscript department (now the Cultural History Archive) with a proposal for the collection of life-stories. Not only was the idea in step with the Cultural History Archive's tradition of collecting memories, but it also resonated with the contemporary emphasis on the rehabilitation of memory; the time was heavy with remembering, gathering and revising of historical memory. The increasing openness of society created optimal conditions for the collection of life-stories. (Hinrikus and Kõresaar 2004, 21)

The time must have been very heavy with remembering, as my perusal of some of these collected and translated life stories tells me. Although it is a very small part of the collection that has been translated into English, yet it is sufficient to show that the "openness" let a torrent of memories burst forth, a torrent that had been forced into silence for a very long time. It is noteworthy here that the initiative to collect started at the end of Soviet rule. It seems there was collective knowledge about the silenced narratives and a collective sense of urgency to narrate and record the same. To me this "collective" was palpable in books and conversations, and its historical significance, urgency, and angst became palpable through the life stories I read. The intensity of what had been collectively withheld although individually endured was such that it could not have lost a moment of the chance to burst forth and reclaim control over individual life and collective reorganization.

Temporality and Spatiality

My representation of Baltic folkloristics as *dramatic* is thus based on methodological plurality that led to multiple sources: the history of the discipline in terms of institutional and individual engagements and works; my conversations with historians, ethnologists, folklorists and archivists; and the life stories of common people as collected/narrated in post-Soviet Estonia, Latvia, and Lithuania. I combine these three to write the history of Baltic folkloristics in the second half of the twentieth century and early twenty-first century, in the historical social context as reflected through the life stories. If one were to write this history of folkloristics only on the basis of folklore scholarship, one would get a record of what happened to folklore scholarship and what the folklore scholars did/collected and published. By engaging this record with the work of ethnologists in the field of life stories and historians, I virtually take the record of folkloristics out of the institutions and place it among the daily life and social context of their country people. In other words, I attempt to understand the folklorists and the folk. It is best to call this an "attempt" as it cannot be comprehensive. This is meant to capture and represent that this is not about folkloristics in ordinary times, but in a "dramatic" phase. This dramatic nature characterized not only folklorists and their institutions, but also the life of the people among whom they did fieldwork. While this required a multidisciplinary approach, it lets us see the disciplinary history of folkloristics not like an insulated tunnel through history, but as fragments in the larger cultural history of people and place. The temporality and the spatiality of folkloristics are taken into consideration as inseparable. Any dramatic event unfolds in time and space; and although it is easier to see that in the confines of theater as compared to the life of nations and peoples, the study of folkloristics in the Baltic countries brought forth the realization that even at the scale of nations and over decades in time, collective life can be dramatic.

CHAPTER TWO

A FLASHBACK

When in 1935 at the congress of the folk-tale investigators at Lund I mentioned
to some friends that the small Estonian people has already collected more
than 70,000 variants of folk-tales, I was answered by way of compliment that
the Estonian people of a million souls was by no means small in the field of
folk-lore, but a promising great power for the investigator hitherto.

—**Oskar Loorits,** *Some Notes on the Repertoire of*
Estonian Folk-Tale. Reprinted in Kuutma and Jaago 2005

Oskar Loorits—the founder of the Estonian Folklore Archives, the
collector of folklore in Livonia (a region in Latvia) and Estonia, and
considered the father of Estonian folkloristics—was doing his major
work at the time the "wars of independence" (Kasekamp 2010, 100)
were being fought in all three Baltic states, but with rather different
sets of circumstances and complexities.

Torn apart by the claims of the Bolshevik Russia and Germany to
rule in Latvia and Estonia and the claims of Poland and Bolshevik
Russia over Lithuania, the Baltic people were fighting to gain independence and establish their independent nations almost for the
first time in modern history. This dramatic sequence started after
World War I when the German occupational forces handed over
the authority to local governments in all the three states. The three
states claimed independence from their prewar and often age-old
foreign rulers. While Estonia managed to gain complete independence from Germans who had ruled there through the medieval

age and whose language continued to have intellectual and cultural significance, Latvia accepted freebooters of the German army to defend its territory from Russia and train its own troops. Lithuania got busy preparing its case for presentation at the Paris Peace Conference. In the meantime, that is, between 1917 and 1919, Estonians fought wars to keep the Red Army off their territory, and so did the Latvians and the Lithuanians with varying degrees of success. Estonia settled difficult negotiations, and Estonia and the USSR became the first countries to recognize each other's existence (Kasekamp 2010, 101). It finally came to the Paris conference to recognize the Baltic states as independent countries.

> In the historical literature the formation of the Baltic states is frequently attributed to the Versailles Treaty, statehood often appears as a gift of the Entente powers wanting a *cordon sanitaire* or buffer zone against Bolshevik Russia. In fact, the peacemakers in Paris in 1919 had faint interest in or knowledge of what was happening in the Baltic region. No one favored the establishment of these independent states except the Estonians, Latvians and Lithuanians themselves. The conflicts in the Baltic region were viewed as peripheral elements of the wider Russian civil war. The Entente powers, particularly the USA and France, preferred to maintain the territorial integrity of the Russian Empire and supported the Russian Whites whose principle was "Russia one and indivisible." Among the many ironies and contradictions in this confusing and complex series of conflicts, where coalitions were fluid and alliances changed overnight, was that the wars of independence were fought partly in alliance with the Russian Whites against the Russian Bolsheviks, who, in the end, were the only ones willing to recognize the right to self-determination of the Baltic nations because they expected that world revolution would soon make nation-states irrelevant. (Kasekamp 2010, 105)

Amidst this turbulence, Loorits, "one of the most influential figures in the Estonian folklore studies of the 1920s and 1930s" began his philological and folklore study at the University of Tartu in 1919 (Västrik 2005, 203). In 1920 he participated in the lengthy fieldwork among the Livonian ethnic group in Latvia. His interest in the folklore and culture of the Livonians, a "small Balto-Finn ethnic group" grew into his massive PhD thesis on the subject (204). Incidentally, Livs were the first tribe subjugated by the German crusaders in 1206 (Kasekamp 2010, 13). The research interest of Loorits had political dimensions—sympathy with the current national consciousness of the Livonians. This sympathy was connected to and extended into the sympathy for the national consciousness in the Baltic states and the raging wars of independence.

Within the context of the Baltic history, Oskar Loorits was focused on something of a far more permanent nature—the oral songs and stories of people in Estonian and Latvian Languages. The lore and the languages that had gone on in spite of the rule of German barons, feudal lords and Teutonic order since the thirteenth century as they had ruled here. The Germans had established feudal order of the medieval ages in these Baltic countries and been the rulers over several Baltic tribes who they also converted to Christianity (Kasekamp 2010, 11–15). "The lands of the Liv, Lettigallian, Selonian, Estonian, Curonian and Semigallians tribes conquered by the German crusaders in the thirteenth century were carved into four bishoprics: Riga, Dorpat, Osel-Wiek and Courland" (31). The system was a form of colonialism that reduced the "native" people of the Baltics to being serfs and subjects in their own lands. One of the relieving features of the German rule had been the early spread and establishment of literacy. As the influence of Martin Luther in the sixteenth century changed the religious landscape of Germany, it also influenced the nature of German rule in Estonia and Latvia. One of these influences was the diminishing of the catholic Teutonic order of monk warriors, and the other was promotion of education by the feudal lords who had come under the influence of Protestant and Calvinist ideologies and felt compelled to support schools and basic education for their serfs, as well as the translation of bible into local languages (40). This promotion of education went a long way in the emergence of a literate populace and establishment of institutions of higher education. Tartu University was established in 1632 and German continued to remain its official language of instruction until World War II. These changes took centuries to manifest themselves, and were further aided by the ruling elite being displaced by the Swedish power in the seventeenth century, which abolished feudalism (51). The power of the German landlords remained, but the lot of the people changed too. Swedish dominance was followed by Russian and there were long periods of conflict between German, Swedish and Russian powers for control of the Baltic through the eighteenth century. The case of Lithuania was somewhat different, as it had been more under the control of the Polish rulers since the medieval ages than German or Russian, although the power struggles continued. Vilnius as a city developed a very special character as a multi-cultural space where the majority was of Jews and Poles, with substantial influence of the Belorussian and German culture and people until the end of World War II (43–44). The nineteenth century was dominated by the Russians and the Baltic countries became part of the Tsarist Empire, which brought in several agrarian reforms and ended serfdom completely (68–69)

By the late nineteenth century, there was an awakening of national consciousness in all three Baltic states, which was the precursor to the spirit of Oskar Loorits. What Loorits was proposing in Lund in 1935 was of significance not only to the folkloristic history, but also to the political history of Estonia and of comparably similar importance to Latvia and Lithuania. The point he was making was the assertion of Baltic languages and cultural expression that had remained outside of the official education, particularly, higher education systems. With the history of domination by foreign powers, the Baltic languages and cultural expression had largely remained in the area of cultural expression termed folklore, that is, not belonging to the ruling classes. It was in the orality and in the countryside that Baltic cultures had continued to survive and grow through the medieval to the modern age. Any cultural identity of the independent countries was unthinkable without conceptualizing language and folklore of the region and without changing the basic paradigms of the education system.

In this context, both the nationalist consciousness and the nationalism in folkloristics were matters hugely different from what these terms implied in the neighboring European countries in the early twentieth century. For example, in Germany, nationalism was about to transform into its ugliest of face—fascism. In the Baltics, it was the definition of freedom from foreign rule and control. The similarity, if at all, could only be found in distant lands, for example, in South Asia in the late nineteenth and early twentieth centuries, where an anticolonial freedom struggle against two centuries of British colonial rule was also employing Indian languages and folklore in the making of the new self-awareness and cultural identity. It is very important to see the context of nationalism to understand its contours and to determine whether it is a positive or a negative force. However, both the Baltics and South Asia seem to have been largely unaware of each other's history and struggle. So, what Loorits was doing had immense local importance, but from today's perspective, it can also be seen as an anticolonial struggle within the context of colonial structures of power within Europe—a subject that has been dwarfed by European colonialism in other continents.

Loorits's publication *"Volkslieder der Liven* (1936) contained 645 Livonian song types, including Livonian original texts and their full translations into German [. . .]. This monumental publication was obviously shaped to support the nation-building of the Livonians, and Loorists planned to follow it with a collection of folk tales" (Västrik, 2005: 205). His engagement with the Livonians, a minority community in Latvia, angered the Latvian state as it disturbed the Latvian nation building of which Livonia was a part, and he was expelled from Latvia in 1937. However, Loorits's activities in Estonia were proceeding at a different rate. He had planned and proposed the making of the Estonian Folklore Archives around 1924. The initial purpose of the archives was to house the manuscript collection of Jakob Hurt, which had been kept in the Finnish Literature Archives in Helsinki. It was also his aim that various small archives or private collections of folklore spread across the country should also be brought under one roof (206).

The work of Jakob Hurt is considered the standard on Estonian folklore, and he is unquestionably the biggest figure in the history of Estonian folkloristics. What he accomplished is indeed awe inspiring in its methodological execution and cultural significance. Hurt was born in 1839, and his higher education and folklore work was done in the second half of the nineteenth century, during the national awakening, and it is in this consciousness that his work is located. He studied theology at Tartu University between 1859 and 1865, at a time when Estonian was not a language of instruction and was taught as a foreign language for those aspiring to be priests. After his education, he worked as a teacher until he became a pastor in 1872 (Jaago 2005, 45). Hurt was one of the people who advocated the use of Estonian language in education, and the collection of folklore included the collection of dialects and increasing the knowledge about Estonian language. The concerns with which he started collecting folklore are encapsulated in his own words, as quoted by Tiiu Jaago:

> Old history books tell us a lot about wars and other external matters in our country, but not about the life of Estonians in this country during times of peace, their works and activities, religion and opinions, their mental life, and generally about everything that a stranger does not notice easily, that nearly does not exist. Here and there in some book, as if unintentionally, a piece has been included, but compared to our own living chronicle and memories of old people, it is like a seed next to a bushel of grain. (Hurt 1879, 19, quoted in 2005, 50)

The concepts "our own living chronicle" and "memories" are important to notice here as these concepts are considered the defining features of his folkloristics. Hurt understood folklore as "folk memories" and therefore saw it always with reference to the past (Jaago 2005, 52). He went about executing his plan of folklore collection in an innovative fashion. His collection of folklore started in 1860 by collecting from family and friends. In 1870, he sent public appeals "for grassroots folklore collection, a method which soon spread throughout Estonia" (58). In 1888, he published an appeal in the newspaper with very precise instructions for collecting dialects and folklore. "Within a year more than 300 volunteers joined the collecting mission, sending in more than a thousand parcels with written records of different types of folklore" (60). This social network not only grew but became a phenomenon causing a cultural consciousness to emerge as also the habit of collecting folklore. Hurt's manuscripts, today the proud possession of the Estonian Folklore Archives in Tartu, are exemplary in many ways: they contain "more than 170 volumes with more than 122,000 pages and more than 260,000 folklore texts amassed from 1860 to 1906" (46). The collection of manuscripts includes detailed information about the collectors and narrators.

No wonder then that Loorits wanted to start the Estonian Folklore Archives by bringing back Hurt's manuscripts from Helsinki. Hurt's collection of Estonian folklore was a great work of scholarship and of equally great service to the awakening of national consciousness. And it is at both these levels that it has remained important, certainly until the very first independent nations were formed in the Baltics, between the two wars.

Loorits worked during this time—between the two world wars and in the first period of independent nationhood for all three Baltic states. As we have seen, his work was deeply connected with national consciousness, yet his world was not only different from that of Hurt; it was also far more complicated. The political significance of folkloristics made it not only an important discipline, but also a very risky enterprise. Loorits was successful in establishing the Folklore Archives, which officially opened in 1927. He also succeeded in bringing back Hurt's manuscripts. This was followed by organizing the archives, training colleagues and assistants, publishing materials, and initiating new collections. Hurt's method of collecting through a network of common people continued, but Loorits expanded the topographical paradigm by paying special attention to collecting folklore of the minority populations of Estonia: Swedes, Finns, Latvians, Germans, Russians, and Gypsies (Västrik 2005, 207). Loorits believed that it was in a combination of all these that the true nature of the Estonian folk, folklore, and cultural history could be understood. Although his approach was mainly rooted in the Finnish historical-geographic method, he "developed a so-called historical-ethnological approach and intended to combine procedures from philology, cultural history, psychology, aesthetics and sociology in the study of folklore" (208). Loorits continued to publish research work in German and Estonian languages, but his texts often came from literary sources and not original folklore texts (210).

What was being accomplished in Estonia between the two world wars had parallels in Latvia and Lithuania. A similar national consciousness was sweeping across the Baltics, and the folklore was like the soul of that national and cultural identity which was bursting forth to express itself and be recognized for itself. In Latvia, too, the current importance was linked to the late nineteenth-century nationalist-cultural awakening and was being institutionalized in the 1920s:

> Precisely during the interwar period, the patriotic duty of collecting and publishing folklore was transformed into a full-fledged, institutionalised academic discipline: the Archives of Latvian Folklore was established; the University of Latvia began offering courses in folkloristics and ethnography, and Latvian folklorists sought a place in the networks of international cooperation flourishing in Europe at that time. The newly established (1918) Latvian nation-state owed its independence to the cultural nationalism of the second half of the

19th century with its strong interest in folklore. Largely, it was the collection of folklore that instigated by the Jaunlatvieši (Young Latvians) movement awakened national consciousness and consolidated people scattered in the borderlands of tsarist Russia in a joint patriotic effort. (Bula 2017)

The Archives of Latvian Folklore was founded in 1924. The nationalist consciousness and zeal that led to this were reflected in three major works by contemporaries of Oskar Loorits: Latvian folksongs, I–VI, 1894–1915, compiled by Krišjānis Barons; Latvian folk legends and tales, I–VII, 1891–1903, collected and published by Ansis Lerhis-Puškaitis; and materials of Latvian folk music, I–VI, 1894–1926, edited by Andrejs Jurjāns. Another very important figure in Latvian folkloristics was Kārlis Straubergs, who enjoyed a position of political power and social status throughout the interwar period. According to Bula (2017), he was the head of the Archives of Latvian Folklore from 1929 through 1944 and author of a large number of works, particularly in the field of mythology. "When 'The Interpretation of Greek Myths and Mythological Theory' appeared in 1926, it was among the very few existent publications about the theoretical aspects of the study of mythology." Straubergs maintained correspondence with several European folklorists and ethnologists, including Loorits.

In Lithuania, too, the movement toward the formation of folklore as a discipline and creation of the institutions of its study had been commensurate with Estonia and Latvia:

Being rooted in the romantic nationalist views of the 19th century, Lithuanian folklore research has ever since experienced all the developments characteristic to folkloristics worldwide, including searching for the "national character" allegedly reflected in folklore, safeguarding of rapidly disappearing relics of the ancient worldview and creativity, establishing authenticity as a key value in folklore, etc. The importance of folklore as national heritage and increase in its collection were particularly notable at the turn of the 20th century, as part and parcel of the national movement inspired by the Lithuanian cultural figure Jonas Basanavičius and his associates [. . .]. Subsequently, viewed by the government of the independent interwar Lithuanian Republic as a matter of national importance and therefore financially supported, folklore collection, publication and research were actively promoted until 1940. (Būgienė 2017, 30)

Oskar Loorits, Kārlis Straubergs, and their contemporaries were living in difficult times, and their nationalism became a threat to their lives as the Russians came back at the end of World War II to occupy the Baltic countries. Both Loorits and Straubergs escaped to Sweden just in time, in 1944. The post–World War II phase of folklore research started in Lithuania on a similar note as that in Estonia and Latvia. Lina Būgienė says that in Lithuania, "with the arrival of the Soviet Union, escape of the Folklore Archive's director Jonas Balys, as also of many others . . . some lost their jobs. Several school teachers who were also folklore collectors" (Būgienė). The most important work of Oskar Loorits, *Grundzüge des estnischen Volksglaubens I–III* was published later in Sweden.

The escape of these scholars and many others has significance beyond their personal lives. It is symbolic of the fact that there were to be many changes in Estonia and in other Baltic countries. This is my research interest—the end of World War II and the establishment of Soviet rule in the Baltics. I am interested in showing the impact of the Soviet rule on folklore studies in the Baltic countries and how that impact has been dealt with since independence of all the three countries in 1991.

CHAPTER THREE

THE DRAMA BEGINS

In 1944, the situation in Estonia was that there had been a tradition of widespread folkloristics research and awareness since the 1880s and growth of institutions in the brief period of independence from 1918 to 1939. The standing of the folkloristics discipline was recognized internationally. On the one hand, this tradition of folkloristics was deeply connected with movements to gain freedom and independence from centuries of rule by foreigners and reclaim linguistic and cultural identity through folklore research. On the other hand, some of the early folklore collectors belonged to those ruling classes, like Baltic Germans. The political implications of Estonian folkloristics were not hidden from anyone and, therefore were plainly visible to the authorities of the USSR which, as one of the victorious Allied powers at the end of World War II, claimed its authority over the Baltic region. Unlike at the end of WWI, not only were the Baltic nations unable to reclaim their independence, but they were further charged with having collaborated with the Nazi German forces during World War II. Although this collaboration, in whatever limited manner, was a strategic means to ward off the control of the USSR, it was enough for the USSR and perhaps the Allied forces to believe that the control of the Baltics by the Soviet Union was correct.

As the Germans retreated and the Red army poured into Baltic territory, Baltic patriots sought to reestablish their independent governments [. . .]. The basis for this hope was the Atlantic Charter, which rejected territorial aggrandizement and supported the principle of national self-determination. This vision of the post-war world agreed upon by the USA and Britain in 1941 was incorporated by the Declaration of United Nations of 1 January 1942 to which USSR was also party. However, the Balts were unaware that at the meeting "the Big Three" in Tehran in 1943, the US president, Franklin D. Roosevelt, and the British prime minister, Winston Churchill, indicated that they would not oppose Stalin's desire to reimpose control over the Baltic states. (Kasekamp 2010, 138)

Whatever the reasons, the Baltic states lost their independence. People representing independent governments were arrested and deposed by the USSR if they did not manage to escape to another country. Resistance to Soviet rule was also organized as underground movements, and thousands of men lost their lives fighting the Red Army. Resistance was strongest in Lithuania, where two hundred thousand died fighting. The resistance movements were crushed brutally until Stalin's death in 1953. After his death, several fighters accepted amnesties offered by the Soviet state, yet resistance continued almost throughout, and the last of the fighters died in the woods in Lithuania in 1986 (Kasekamp, 2010: 142). Many more citizens left for refuge in other countries. "Altogether more than 140,000 Latvians, 75,000 Estonians and 65,000 Lithuanians fled their homeland" (139). Such was the fear of rule by the Soviet Union as experienced from 1939 through 1941. Soviet control was established over all the three Baltic countries of Latvia, Lithuania, and Estonia in 1944 and lasted until 1991. Henceforth began the drama of which the following were the first three acts.

Act 1: Censoring

Right after the war, Soviet authorities took full control of the Estonian Folklore Archives. During the war, the most important task had been to save the manuscript materials from the threat of destruction. The collections had therefore been shifted to various rural locations. After the war, "the directives" started arriving from Moscow. The first one, giving orders to find and separate all the manuscripts "that are not necessary for the Literary Museum or contain anti-Soviet materials" arrived on May 12, 1945, and was signed by Elena Pavlova, head of the Museum Sector of the Peoples Commissariat for Education. More precise instructions followed [. . .]. The first wave of censorship lasted from 1945 to 1946. Most of the manuscripts were checked during this time." This was no mean task. "Checking the folklore collections was more difficult than going through the contents of the libraries and archives. Every single piece of folklore needed to be read, its content analyzed (ideally in the context of its creation), and aspects of the time of its collection and people connected to it needed to be taken into consideration. As the collections were very large, checking the contents was even more difficult" (Kulasalu 2013, 70).

The work itself had to be carried out by the staff and researchers of the archive. Risto Järv, director of the Estonian Folklore Archives, said that the Soviet authorities

wanted to continue folklore work but to change the old conceptions . . . not to have folklore collected by people who left Estonia, not to collect some part of folklore and third part was that archive should collect and publish new kind of folklore, that is useful to the soviet regime . . . so we had to look for new kinds of materials like, socialistic proverbs . . . It was written to please find these kind of materials . . . that older kind of material was controversial . . . ideologically very big. . . . Workers from the Archive had to do it [censoring]. So communist party had instruction, but in Estonia, archivists themselves had to do it and then say that it is done, and now ok to show materials to researchers. . . . It was not people from outside, but inside who had to do the censorship.

The work was periodically supervised, but the most important form of supervision or ensuring compliance to the directives was the terror that had been generated by the demonstration of the state's capacity for ruthless repression. This is a subject to which we shall return, but for now, the process of censorship itself is under focus. More recent collections were checked more thoroughly than the older ones. Jakob Hurt's collection, for example, was not checked at all, perhaps because it was too old to be politically problematic. However, the collection of Mathias Johann Eisen—the other important collector along with Hurt and who followed Hurt's model, was thoroughly investigated. Newer collections (compiled during World War II and German occupation) were checked for political reasons, like censoring any positive depiction of bourgeoisie or nationalism, but also for moralistic reasons, like censoring "obscenities."

Both newer and older collections were mainly checked for obscenities in texts and motifs. "However, in general, to find anything obscene meant attentive reading of all the manuscripts. The censorship practices of obscene texts show, therefore, how thoroughly collections needed to be checked and the struggles of the employees with this job show how demanding the task was" (Kulasalu 2013, 71). The state reduced the staff and the researchers working in the archives to people not only following the directives to censor and manipulate folklore materials, but to do it to the best of their ability so as not to experience repression themselves. Fear of repression ensured compliance by the staff. And in spite of that, repression took place. Folklorists Herbert Tampere, Rudolf Poldmae, and August Annist were arrested. Loorits escaped to Sweden in 1944, so his photos were removed, and his works were banned and censored.

Methods for censoring were the following: "[The texts] were either redacted with ink, paper was glued over them or pages were cut out. On one of the first pages of the manuscripts, the person checking it made a note of her or his name, the date and the numbers of pages that were cut out" (Kulasalu 2013, 71). The sheets cut were kept separately in the Department of Special Storage and were returned to the Department of Folklore in the later decades, but they were not allowed to be added to the original materials. More such sheets were discovered by the archives staff in 2002.

The last wave of checking and censoring happened in 1953, and then it stopped. By then, however, the context of the archives had changed. So, Oskar Loorits, who had established the Folklore Archives, was certainly hearing of these processes sitting in Sweden. He continued to work on Estonian folklore, produced his seminal work, and kept the advocacy for the study of Baltic folkloristics on in the free Western world. His homeland, the archives, and the study and research on folklore were in completely new circumstances. Reflecting on the question as to why it was so important for the Soviet authorities to control the archival folklore materials, Kaisa Kulasalu says in a more recent publication,

> Among other things, the content and purposes of memory institutions were evaluated and re-established. As Jacques Derrida has claimed, there can be no proper political control without a control over archives and memory (1996, 4). Control over texts shapes behaviours and discourses. In Soviet ideas, the distance between a text and reality was a very short one. The texts were representing reality and at the same time, their content was seen as something that will shape reality (Lõhmus 2002, 18). The main arguments behind censoring and viseuring the collections of memory institutions could be described as follows: The purpose of archives is to recreate past. Changing the organisation of memory institutions changes the ways people are communicating with their past. The goal of changes is to create some kind of world order. (2017, 134)

Act 2: Purging

The ideological paraphernalia being the same all across the Baltics, actually across the Soviet Union, it is interesting to see whether the processes were exactly duplicated everywhere. To understand this,

I met with folklorists in Riga, Latvia, and Vilnius, Lithuania. In Latvia, the situation was somewhat different, as Dace Bula told me in a conversation:

> This is one striking case, and one difference from Estonia; they had this censoring of the Archives like sticking of pages etc. This didn't happen here in Latvia. Archives were never closed. It functioned. Of course, it was not advisable to collect anti-Soviet jokes or anti-Soviet materials, but we can find even this kind of material, which is very striking. Old collections were not censored. Yes, some of the main figures of inter-war folkloristics emigrated in 1944, like Kārlis Straubergs, Ludis Bērziņš, Arveds Švābe. It was not advisable to reprint their works or use them for your research works. Their names did not appear in encyclopedias, etc. but they were still on the shelves of libraries or archives, not all of them, but most of them were freely available.

The difference is important in itself, but it is noteworthy that a latent threat was somehow communicated. When Bula says that it was not "advisable" to do certain things, she is referring to the common knowledge about the possibility of repressive action by the authorities. This feeling of "being watched" existed everywhere. It is not possible to ascertain how this feeling was created, but it is imaginable that it was created due to the overall atmosphere of lack of freedom, of reprisals and perhaps some knowledge of what was happening elsewhere. This feeling is actually far more important than the actual acts of repression, as this is the evidence of the fear of the state. We shall see in the following how this feeling leads to a certain kind of scholarly writing.

Writing about this new circumstance in Latvia in a volume published in 2017, Bula tells us,

> What happened to the rest of the authorities of Latvian interwar folkloristics? [. . .] For those who stayed in Soviet Latvia, life was far from favourable. They got and lost jobs, they were persecuted for their

"bourgeois-nationalist" past, they were forced to renounce their previous publications, [. . .] even though the founder of the Archives of
Latvian Folklore Anna Bērzkalne (1891–1956) set to explore the images
of Stalin and Lenin in Soviet folk-songs [. . .]. There were no means
to ensure disciplinary continuity. (47)

So, the reality was not very different for those living and working in Riga or in Tartu. Anna Bērzkalne (1891–1956) is indeed an
important figure here. Not only was she the founder of the Latvian
Archives, but she was a woman of unprecedented achievement in
her generation. Rita Treija has written on this remarkable folklorist of Latvia: "Bērzkalne directed the Archives of Latvian Folklore
during its 'start up' period" (Rita Treija, 2017). While she was sci-
entifically committed to the Finnish historic-geographical school,
her commitment to folklore was born of a nationalist spirit. In
1925, she wrote a brochure for folklore collectors, which was widely
circulated.

The text, in places, challenged the reader by appealing to Latvian folklore collectors' patriotic feelings: "The voluminous published collections of folk traditions, which we have always been so proud to present
to other countries, turn out to be insufficient for researching our
folklife and poetry, not to mention the fact that our northern Finnish
neighbours and especially Estonians have defeated us ten times over as
far as the quantity of folklore collected" (1925: [1]). This admission un-
deniably positioned research about folk spiritual heritage as a national
duty, to be executed without delay, especially in those regions where
little had been collected. The pathos of the proclamation encouraged
everyone to get involved: "later it will be a source of great shame if
because of our negligence, recklessness, and spiritual inertia, we have
allowed the riches of our fathers' fathers to perish" (1925: [3]). Bērzkalne made an effort to acquaint the popular readership with the pos-
sibilities for using the comparative method of the historic-geographic
school for such research. The original 3000 copies of the brochure had

all been distributed by 1927 because of abundant public interest. The Archives of Latvian Folklore decided to publish a condensed version in the newspaper. (Rita Treija, 2017)

In a conversation with me, Rita Treija said, "1947–1953, until Stalin's death—that was the harshest period. Since she [Anna Bērzkalne] was a representative of the Finnish school, harsh criticism was forced against her via mass media, via anonymous letters. She was a new doctor, she could work but she can't work because of ideological circumstances. And well, pretty sad story. Anna Bērzkalne suffered the most, that's my opinion."

The case of Anna Bērzkalne highlights what Soviet repression was on individuals who had not escaped in 1944. While she was a known nationalist in the interwar period, she could not be trusted because her nationalist feelings might transform folklore research into rebellious activity against the USSR. Anna Bērzkalne was intelligent enough to realize the shift that had taken place and tried to practice her method under new names and even collect folklore about Stalin and communism.

Toms Ķencis tells us of yet another aspect in the survival strategies of Latvian scholars in the act of declaring a change of consciousness that they had experienced:

[P]ublic self-criticism was a cultural ritual practice characteristic of Stalinist society: it was performed in purges of the Russian Communist Party in the 1930s as well as in scientific circles of the 1940s and 1950s. Scholars gave special lectures where they acknowledged their contamination with reactionary theories and accepted the official doctrine. In Soviet Russia, Propp renounced formalism, Andreyev the Finnish method, and Sokolov the vulgar sociology of Hans Naumann (cf. Dorson 1963). Also in Soviet Latvia, in 1948, Bērzkalne, the leading follower of the Finnish school, gave the lecture "My current and previous methods in folklore" with the purpose to claim Marxism Leninism as her real choice. (2017, 156).

Ķencis goes on to say that this was indeed not an easy route as "it meant doing research with knowledge that your former colleagues might have been tortured and shot in prison or sent to labour camps in Siberia" (157). Bērzkalne was also not able to gain the trust of the communist state. If we look more closely, an unethical and hypocritical ideological orientation was being forced upon the scholars.

Act 3: Constructing Folklore

Another aspect of this forced orientation was the directive to collect folklore about the Soviet Union, Soviet leaders, and the collective-farms (*kolkhoz*) system, and, obviously, this folklore had to be in praise of all these subjects. On the one hand, folklore was important for the Soviet authorities, since Maxim Gorky in 1934 had "stressed the optimism in folklore and the value of it for studying social relations" (Kulasalu 2017, 140). On the other hand,

> Joseph Stalin himself warned that "Old customs and habits, traditions and prejudices that are inherited from the old society, are the most dangerous enemy of socialism [. . .]. Therefore, the struggle against these traditions and customs, their mandatory overcoming in all fields of our work, and ultimately the education of new generations according to the spirit of socialism—these are the current tasks of our party; without carrying them out, the victory of socialism is impossible. (Ķencis 2017, 158)

This implied that, at one level, one had to look for and highlight the class consciousness of the toiling masses in the traditional folklore and, on another level, look for "new" folklore.

The agenda of science was constructing rather than representing reality or, in other words, the objectivity of research was measured not by its impartiality, but the opposite—its partiality in the socialist struggle. The struggle against old traditions took place on multiple levels: from

prohibitions of traditional festivities and religious practices to censorship of pre-war folklore collections (cf. case of Estonian Archives
of Folklore—Kulasalu 2013). Part of this struggle was the invention of
new traditions and folklore, authenticated and legitimised by academic research afterwards. The implementation of total politics in
academic practices demanded a strictly defined theoretical framework.
Overall, it was constituted by a specific modification of Marxism-Leninism. (Ķencis 2017, 159)

The Soviet authorities promoted collectivization in folklore
research also and sent "expeditions" of several scholars to collect
folklore instead of promoting individual researchers—a subject to
which we shall return in the chapter on folklore archives (Kulasalu
2017, 143). In the first decade after the takeover by the USSR and
while Stalin was alive, the insistence on "new folklore" produced
some weird results. Some examples of such folklore constructed by
traditional performers for the sake of researchers are cited by Toms
Ķencis (2017; LFK refers to the Archives of Latvian Folklore):

Oh, brother, kind and sweet,
Let your sister join the kolkhoz!
Kolkhoz means an easy life,
Work is done while singing songs. (LFK 1842, 4093) (163)

I am weaving a crown
From flowers and from leaves,
Which I will put on the head
Of our Stalin;
He has grown for us
Like a great oak,
We hang from its branches
Like small acorns. (LFK 1856, 1) (164)

Many are friends that I have
Many are brothers that I have

In vast Russia:

I can go visiting,

In the south and the north. (LFK 1769, 2349) (165)

Ķencis considers the last example to "be a poor adaptation of a classical song, or it was based on a subversive strategy, ironically referring to mass deportations to 'vast Russia' in 1941 and 1949." He also cites some "new Soviet proverbs": "Where is Stalin, there is victory" (LFK 1860, 1939); "The Soviet man can do anything" (LFK 1850, 7707); "The collective is our heart" (LFK 1850, 6661); "The kolkhoz leads to a happy life" (LFK 1850, 7946); "What man cannot do alone, people can do together" (LFK 1850, 1600); "Less talk, more work" (LFK 1850, 7952); "Labour: the basis of our happiness" (LFK 1860, 1852)" (165). According to Kulasalu (2017, 147), in the Setomaa region of Estonia, Seto singers were also producing such new folklore.

And yet, in spite of the pressure by the authorities, not much new folklore could be produced by the researchers. This led to further tightening of the controls (Kulasalu 2017, 141). However, the practice of looking for new Soviet folklore came to an end with the death of Stalin in 1953 (Ķencis 2017, 166).

In the decades following the 1950s, the day-to-day reality became more stable, as people knew the repressive nature of the state and tried to adjust to it. This stability was not the deeper reality, and sometimes the banal and the deeper reality came face to face for the Balts. This is evident in the study and research on folklore, which were neatly divided between the university and the archives, respectively. The study was pursued at the university, and the research, in and by the archives. We will follow this process in the next chapter.

CHAPTER FOUR

RESISTANCE SITE 1

Folklore at the University

After the death of Stalin in 1953, the severity of the USSR forces somewhat changed. Soviet rule became an everyday reality. Although this seems easier than the times of deportations, it was rather tough. One had to follow the rules at every moment of every day as any lapse could bring reprisals of different kinds. New rules were designed in Moscow every now and then, and everyone was expected to follow them. This applied to university teaching and learning as well. What was to be taught, how it was to be taught and learned, and what was right or wrong were clearly spelled out. On top of the rules was surveillance of whether the rules were being followed. So, one had to be very careful, particularly at the workplace. Based on the experiences of some of the people I conversed with, in this chapter, we will see how teaching and learning of folklore went on at the universities. This chapter is based mainly on the Estonian experience, where the university houses the largest department of folklore studies in Europe.

The Double Role

The study of folklore at the university was to be guided by the Marxist-Leninist perspective, but the way teaching and learning functioned in reality was not exactly the way the state imagined it would be. Indeed, there was the imposition of the Russian language: students had generally already learned it in school, and PhD dissertations were to be written in Russian, as I was told by such scholars as Ülo Valk, Kristin Kuutma, and Tiiu Jaago. These three scholars received their educations during the Soviet period. They got to have a feel of the educational institutions before the Soviet times through their teachers, mainly through university professors. Kristin Kuutma told me that she chose not to pursue a PhD owing to the compulsions, including the compulsion to go to Moscow for the viva voce examination before the award of the degree. Estonians in general were reluctant to travel to Russia owing to several concerns, some of which will become clear in the following conversation with Tiiu Jaago. Jaago earned her PhD in 1990—just when the Soviet power began to crumble—and hers was the first PhD in ethnology to be allowed to be written in Estonian. Her viva voce was also held at the University of Tartu. Kristin Kuutma earned her PhD in the United States after Estonia became an independent nation in 1991. Tiiu Jaago and Kristin Kuutma both talked to me in some detail about their experiences, and in the following I will analytically present the content of their conversations with me.

Jaago theorized the experience of folklore study at the university in the early 1980s by saying there existed "two worlds" simultaneously and of the practice of "parallel knowledge" systems. According to her, it was very important for the Estonian students to have professors "who knew the time before the Soviet time, and in this way it was parallel knowledge." For her, this teacher was the folklorist Eduard Laugaste (1909–1994) who, while teaching folklore within the prescribed format, communicated to the students knowledge about *Estonian* culture and folklore. It is important to remember that any insistence on "Estonian" was considered nationalist and anti-Soviet in nature. Jaago had apologized to me in advance for her "limited" knowledge of the English language, but, in fact, her English was very good. However, her statements were regularly peppered with "if you can understand me" or "if you know what I mean" or, more directly, "Can you understand me?" These idiomatic expressions connected us across great distances, as my response would clearly show her whether and how far I "understood" her. In our case, understanding was not only a linguistic matter, but it referred to the realties that were under discussion: whether, for example, I, as an Indian, could understand the atmosphere of the Soviet period, the need for secrecy, the ways in which teachers subverted the prescriptions of the state, and the ways in which Estonians communicated with each other. Indeed, the very concept of parallel knowledge was referring to a very nuanced and complex form of communication.

Jaago gave two examples of how Eduard Laugaste practiced this "parallel knowledge." She told me that one day he came to class with a Russian newspaper. "It was written in it that culture exist[s] only during Russian culture, but he said Estonian culture not only exist[s] in Russian time, but Estonian culture does not exist. . . . They did not recognize Estonian culture." What Jaago is referring to here is the way *culture* was understood in the Soviet Union. In theory, the USSR believed in self-determination of nations, but for Stalin, it meant development of cultures "national in form and socialist in content," which would ultimately be merged into "One General Culture." The concept for this was *Sliyanie (fusion)*, which meant merging all with Russian language and the creation of *homo sovieticus*—an individual with no homeland, ready to be assigned to work in any part of the USSR. A pop song of the Brezhnev era that says, "My address is no house or street, my address is the Soviet Union," propagated this idea of culture and cultural identity (Kasekamp 2013, 158). So, by bringing the Russian newspaper in the classroom and reading a piece that propagated the idea of culture as conceived in Moscow and to be adopted by all, Laugaste was making his Estonian students aware of how their "Estonian" identity was being denied by the state. He then proceeded to teach them Estonian folklore that had existed since before the Soviet period. Jaago said that through such oblique references she understood as a student that the preferred theoretical paradigm of the Estonian scholars was the Finnish historical-geographical method, while, in Russia, it was structuralism.

> I actually understood that something happened in folkloristic philoso-
> phy . . . Laugaste was representative of Finnish school . . . you know it
> . . . It was very methodological . . . It might seem different in Russia . . .
> In Estonia it was Finnish school . . . In Russia it was structuralism . . .
> you understand . . . I understood that it was not very good . . . frame
> for us to visit Russia conferences. They didn't take us seriously. At that
> time, Finnish school was in conflict with structuralism . . . It was . . . In
> this way I understood . . . that it was not correct for folklore research
> . . . that we did not use good methods.

Jaago was living between the two worlds—a unique hermeneutic situation with regards to the specific contours of the occupation of Estonia by the Soviet Union.

The other example she gave me of parallel knowledge was when she wanted to write her master's dissertation on an illustrator of children's books, Laugaste advised her, "Think different. Take other material, like fairytales of Julius Magiste." Jaago had gone to school during Soviet times, but Laugaste was advising her to study the texts of a pre-Soviet Estonian folklorist, an apparently harmless choice in the eyes of the state, but an opportunity to connect with materials that were not highlighted by the educational institutions. Magiste was a folklorist during the war and had moved to Sweden. Jaago said of Laugaste that "he gave research topics to people in my generation to visit these hidden archives . . . I think it is in this way the parallel world worked in this time." The "hidden archives" refers to the materials that were not part of the canonized education and until specifically approached would not come to the notice of the students. Laugaste was making the students use the little space they had to choose their research topics to study pre-Soviet Estonian folklore collections. Much of his strategies must have become clear to Jaago only later, but when they did, they led her to theorize upon the intellectual world under the Soviet Union as a world of parallel knowledge systems. This is a brilliant way of portraying the art of subversion in the everyday world of compliance under a repressive state.

The Bigger Scene

My conversation with Jaago took place on June 14, 2016. June 14 is a day of historic importance to the Baltics because on the night of June 14, 1941 the worst form of oppression—mass deportations to Siberia—by the USSR was unleashed in Estonia, Latvia, and Lithuania. She showed me the black ribbons on Estonian flags flying at half-mast on all the buildings. In June in the Baltic countries, the nights hardly ever turn dark, so they are called "white nights." Two days after our conversation, I traveled through the night and was mesmerized by the beauty of the white nights and wondered what those who were picked up from their homes and deported to Siberia saw seventy-five years earlier. It was the knowledge of those deportations that made people cautious about following rules but also brave and conscious about the need for subversion.

The historian Andre Kasekamp talks of this culture of "subversion of russification" by intellectuals, artists, and writers. The latter, artists and writers, were organized in unions and were supported by the state. They were also very respected in society. There were many books published in the Soviet period. The phenomenon of voracious readers in the time is noteworthy too. Artists and writers used this space in creative ways to bypass the otherwise repressive guidelines. Poetry was a popular form as censorship could be more easily subverted here; poets and dramatists wrote about old historical Baltic figures and employed folk motifs to subvert russification. All attempts by the state to stop midsummer festivities were not successful. The Balts fought for and gained permission for organizing every five years an open-air summer festival that had huge audiences and thousands of singing choirs. Although these activities were carefully scrutinized (for example, singing was aimed at promoting the singing of socialist songs extolling the virtues of socialism), a lot slipped in, and thus the Balts clung to their culture and language (Kasekamp 2010, 158–59). We shall see later how singing became a major form of protest in 1990.

The Undercurrent

Ülo Valk became a faculty member in the 1980s, before the fall of the Soviet Union experienced the university system of folkloristics in the Soviet times. He believed that on "a daily basis there was not much to do. Since there was no connection with the foreign scholarship and journals, books etc. there was little to read and discuss. One came to office and remained there the whole day as required, did just what was required and nothing more, because 'more' could get one into trouble. The only good aspect of the Soviet system was that it permitted and funded the discipline of folklore study throughout its rule. As such it considered folklore an important subject." This is indeed an important point, that the USSR funded and continued the study of folklore. At the university level, it ensured the continued existence of folklore departments like that of the University of Tartu, where the persistence of the infrastructure helped them revive and regenerate quickly when freedom arrived. On the other hand, the study of folklore within the prescribed limits also played a role in dealing with the repressive nature of the state.

The study of folklore at the university under the Soviet rule was a space where students had a chance to connect with Estonian/ Latvian/Lithuanian language and culture without using the term "national" in reference to language and culture. This was of crucial importance in maintaining the sense of distinct cultural identity that was being ironed out by the socialist state policies. The cultural identity was seen as divisive and as threat to the existence of the Soviet Republic. Folklore became the undercurrent of the calm on the surface, which was maintained at the day-to-day level by not questioning or criticizing the state and following the instructions received. The undercurrent kept alive exactly that which the state feared—the sense of distinct cultural identity. The power of this undercurrent will become visible in late 1980s when the USSR started losing its control. The fact that Tiiu Jaago wrote her PhD dissertation in Estonian and had the defense in Tartu shows that the wish to do so was already there, and the moment it seemed possible, it was done. In spite of decades of imposition of the Russian language, the undercurrent for the assertion of "own" languages was strong and ready to come up to the surface.

The study of folklore under the Soviet rule was divided into the university departments and the archives. The university departments were expected to teach, and the archives were to do the active collection and preservation of folklore. In the following chapter, we will see what role the folklore archives played in the three Baltic countries.

CHAPTER FIVE

RESISTANCE SITE 2

The Folklore Archives

The folklore archives in all three Baltic countries were established in 1920s, that is, in the interwar period when all three nations were free countries. The establishment of the folklore archives as public institutions recognized the existing scholarship that had been in the making since the nineteenth century and before freedom and enabled the institutionalization of both big and small private collections. It was in this process that Jakob Hurt, a Baltic German and pioneer collector of folklore in nineteenth century Estonia, became a national figure. The establishment of the folklore archives by the free countries also gave a clear sign that folklore was central to the idea of "national culture". The importance of the establishment is still evident; for example, the new building of the Estonian National Museum that opened in 2016 has Jakob Hurt's bust right behind the entry; the Archives of Latvian Folklore is housed in the prestigious National Library that opened in 2014, and the Lithuanian Folklore Archives is housed in the Institute of Lithuanian Literature and Folklore. It is because of this importance the Soviet authorities kept them under tight control. We have seen in the second chapter how the archives were censored, although differently in each country. In this chapter, we will discuss how the lives of scholars and institutions continued once the Soviet rule had become more stable. This chapter is almost entirely based on Latvian and Lithuanian folklore archives.

The Expeditions: The Latvian Experience

I first heard of the folklore research "expeditions" on May 30, 2016, from Baiba Krogzeme-Mosgorda in the Archives of Latvian Folklore in Riga. After showing me the new infrastructure for the folklore archive and research in the recently opened National Library that dominates the landscape on the left bank of the Daugava River, Krogzeme-Mosgorda sat down with me in her office to talk about folklore research in Latvia under the Soviet rule. She had been a researcher in the same archives and knew the times well. I had also just seen the huge amounts of materials that were collected in those decades and are now housed in the archives. Krogzeme-Mosgorda told me about the expeditions:

The archives filed the research projects and presented plans to document folklore in a certain region to the local authorities. These plans were seen and approved by various agencies, including the local Communist Party leaders. They were approved in a collaborative manner with other disciplines. Once approved, a big group of folklorists, ethnologists, linguists, historians, geographers, and other disciplines went on an *expedition* together to conduct field research in a certain region. For this expedition, funds, transport, accommodation in the field etc. was provided for by the state. The expeditions took place in the summer and every participant was very enthusiastic about it. So a lot of materials were collected. The technology for collection was also provided, which was generally state-of-the-art, and in 1980s bulky video cameras were also provided. At the end of the expedition there was a festival organized to which the folk performers were invited to perform and local authorities and communist party members also attended. The collected materials were brought back to the archives and then began the process of transcribing, archiving, and publication. These expeditions were very good and interesting and gave the researchers an opportunity to document folklore in abundance without the burden of managing project funds. The chosen region too got studied from various disciplinary perspectives.

We had this conversation on a very warm, sunny day, and behind Krogzeme-Mosgorda, was an open green field and a busy road in the historic city. I returned to the archives again in May 2017 and was introduced to Aldis Pūtelis, Guntis Pakalns, Dace Bula, Beatrise Reidzāne, and Māra Vīksna. Rita Treija, Baiba Krogzeme-Mosgorda, and Toms Ķencis were already known to me, and we talked again.

Beatrise Reidzāne and Māra Vīksna joined the archives when Soviet rule was well established, around 1970. They shared their experience of this time when "national" cultures were not so forcefully suppressed as under Stalin. The other side of the reality was that people had learned to live with the situation and knew what was permitted and what was not. Beatrise Reidzāne told me, "To work on mythology research was out of borders." She went on to say, "You need to have some allowance from [someone] higher. It is nationalism. And Soviet international science was against any nationalism. So, Folklore . . . how to say . . . is a very *dangerous* science. You need to look not to say that you have something better in your folklore, or something different from other folklore. Some folklore was higher . . . Russian is the highest level, and all others under this level" (May 29, 2017). Talking about the main characteristic of being a folklorist in Soviet times, Māra Vīksna said, "You could not do what you wanted. For example, you could have wished to study folksongs or folk beliefs but that was inappropriate. There is no such thing as folk belief. One had to collect more recent songs, not classic folksongs— it was not favorable to record them" (Māra Vīksna, on May 29, 2017, spoke in Latvian, interpreted consecutively by Aldis Pūtelis).

"Mythology" was a particularly problematic area of study under the Soviet rule as it was seen as part of religion. "Soviet Latvian research into mythology is constituted by a subordination of myth as a phenomenon of religion, to myth as ideology. The power imbalance in Soviet knowledge production apparatus is reflected in the same way: the Communist Party, drawing its legitimisation from Marxist-Leninist science, dictates truth to the sciences. Rephrasing Bacon: in this system power is knowledge rather than vice versa" (Ķencis 2012, 153).

And while mythology was problematic, religion was taboo. In Estonia, the Soviet scholarship on language and culture emphasized the pre-Christian past of the people, and "[f]olklore was conceptualized as a manifestation of pre-literary peasant culture that would now finally disappear because of general social progress: the official ideology saw both folk-belief and religion in general as superstitious survivals and obstacles on the road to Communism" (Valk and Kulmar 2015, 5).

On the one hand, it was clear to researchers what should or should not be researched. On the other hand, they constantly subverted and tested the limits of the state's power. Innovative thinking was a way of subverting the state's control: for example, being innovative in coining new names to methods and materials. So, "mythological" songs would become included under more acceptable categories. It is noteworthy here that in Latvian folklore studies, songs are the main component. The state had demanded methodological changes: while pre-Soviet folksong collections were organized as per rituals and occasions of singing, new collections had to be organized along "work" categories, and folksongs were to be mainly seen as work songs. This meant that songs that mentioned a particular work group would be grouped together even if they were performed on different occasions. Since in mythological stories working groups are also mentioned, collectors started placing them in new categories.

An example of the researchers testing the limits of the state's tolerance was the organization of midsummer or summer solstice festivities, an old custom in the Baltic countries when on the night of June 23, bonfires are lit, and people stay out the whole night and enjoy family and community life. Māra Vīksna and Beatrise Reidzāne were the two who thought that they should try to organize this national festival again, and since it is not religious, it should not be a problem. So they spoke with an acquaintance who was the headmaster of a village school to use the premises. He agreed, and they spread the word. Between 150 and 200 people gathered there, including some

Lithuanian friends. During the festival, the secret police showed up, and Beatrise Reidzāne, Māra Vīksna, and others, including the headmaster, were taken to the KGB office, where they had to admit what an anti-Soviet activity they had organized and that it was a crime. Everyone received some form of punishment, and the headmaster of the school was sacked. Reidzāne was "exiled" from the Folklore Section to the Linguistic Section. "It was some exile for me, to go from fifteenth-floor Folklore to thirteenth-floor Linguist[ic]s, where my job was checking the vocabulary of literary language. We had forbidden writers. My first job was to take out quotations of their works from this dictionary." Baiba Krogzeme-Mosgorda and Aldis Pūtelis told me that this was a regular form of repression—to move someone from one organization to another.

These memories are reflective of a peculiar time marked by a culture of permissions and restrictions. The "don'ts" outnumbered the "dos" generally; and even then, to do the dos, people required prior permission from the authorities. Guntis Pakalns told me, "Soviet time was this eternal time, what is allowed, where is the limit, what happens if you reach the limit" (May 29, 2017). And yet, the fact of repression was constantly being subverted. Baiba Krogzeme-Mosgorda studied in 1980s and said that mythology was a popular interest because it was prohibited. She wrote her master's thesis on the thunder god. However, not all were lucky enough to get away with it. Māra Vīksna and Aldis Pūtelis told me of a PhD dissertation on orphans, fully written, but upon submission not accepted because the subject was not nice for the state. Pūtelis reasoned sarcastically, "Because orphans were just out, it was a happy country. There were no orphans or disabled people in the Soviet society!"

People learned to avoid certain subjects or hide them under acceptable nomenclature and finally add a line or two from Stalin's or Lenin's works in the introduction to their research work. Vīksna said, "So the actual attitude was something like that—no one ever accepted it [the party's demand] so truly, but ... if you look at actual written words, they [quotes from Stalin and Lenin] are there." Bula told me, "Well, they did this lip service by starting their writings or books with reference to Stalin's or Lenin's works, but that was a very thin layer of rhetoric. The main study was devoted to classical folklore genres, to history of Latvian folkloristics etc." Strategies were required again at the time of publication because every book was approved at various levels and checked for its content. One of the concerns of the people checking was how these materials could be seen in the light of Marxist-Leninist thought, that how the materials themselves could legitimize the ideas of Marx and Lenin about "people" and their world. Krogzeme-Mosgorda told me, "In the preface or introductions to the collections of folklore the authors did not forget to mention Marx and Lenin and to definitely cite something from Lenin's writing. They tried to attach that interpretation to the materials that would make the collection acceptable for publication." And once the acceptance came, publication was not a problem as the Soviet state published a lot of books. So, it made sense to collect, transcribe and publish folklore collections, as analytical and interpretative scholarship was more difficult to get acceptance and might even have put the scholars to risk of repression for their views. One had to play safe when it came to expression of *views*.

Behind this thin layer of rhetoric was the engagement with the past, that is, with the history of culture, and a rather intense one. Bula explained to me why: "This 'past of the field' was [a] kind of escape from things going on around them." That is not very surprising, given the atmosphere of repression. While it is rather clear to those who lived under it, others might want to know how exactly this repression functioned. The secret police of course had the job of keeping an eye on people. On the open level, there were Communist Party members at every level of administration who were supposed to advise and supervise people. People like these, for example, could inform on the organization of the mid-summer festivities. On the other hand, Bula said, "When you go for field work and let's say there is a kolkhoz, collective farm there, there is a group of communist party members and they organized a meeting and folklorists went there and documented what is being talked there during this meeting and we have those materials from the early 1950s. Conversations going on during these meetings have been documented." So the folklorists were themselves expected to consult with the local party members regarding the collection of folklore in their area.

We can say that the network of the state was the network of social relations too, and it is within the boundaries of these that one was permitted to function. On the subject of boundaries—even the national borders constituted a separate category. So, more special permissions were needed for the collection of folklore in the border area. Even to the USSR people were not free to travel. Thus, the participation of Lithuanians in the summer festivities mentioned above was a major problem. "You could not go to Estonia and say I am a scientist from Riga and want to look at your materials and speak to you, but you had to get some supervisor from high and then go and speak to 'communist' scientist," said Beatrise Reidzāne. The sense of sarcasm, far more palpable in the spoken words, that in the transcribed quotations here, refers to the prevalent paradigm that scholars had to be Communists too or be seen as Communists by the state.

In this situation, expeditions were a great a relief as one was permitted to do something. "Expeditions happened, but they were prepared. In our folklore program it was compulsory to go on expedition. Two weeks of folklore expedition, two weeks of language/dialect expedition . . . I was in [the] eastern part of Latvia to do this job, and we collected folklore. We had the materials given to the Latvian folklore archives" (Beatrise Reidzāne). These collections made during the Soviet period constitute the largest part of the Lithuanian Folklore Archives today. In a lighter vein, Māra Vīksna told me how four jokes once ended up in the collection: two were about the president of free Latvia in 1930s, and two, about Lenin. The jokes about Lenin were promptly removed, and the jokes about the Latvian president were archived. One was not allowed to joke about Lenin or Stalin. Aldis Pūtelis, the interpreter for Vīksna, added his own joke: "Do you know which is the highest building in Latvia? The KGB building: one can see Siberia from there." He also laughed, saying that all those jokes about Lenin and Stalin must still be available in the KGB archives.

As these expeditions were conducted along with visual documentation, there are a lot of photographs available. One wonders whether the visual document may reveal some hidden aspects of the reality, but the photos seem to be very cautious and preplanned: researchers with people, people as portraits with not much visible background, people posing in traditional costumes, and so on. It seems that the photographers were using similar strategies as those of the authors writing their introduction. Photos had to be true to the *socialist idea* of people. So only *views* were taken or printed that did not land the photographer or the people in trouble. In all probability, the photos archived were also a selection by some authority from the photos shot.

Today, the city Riga has regained its glory, and an important symbol of that regeneration is the National Library itself; interestingly, it is designed on the folktale idea of the glass mountain. The website of the library says,

> It was designed by the internationally renowned Latvian architect *Gunnar Birkerts* to be both a striking architectural symbol for Latvia and a multi-functional structure that meets the needs of a modern information based society [. . .]. In Latvian folklore, a crystal mountain symbolizes the height of achievement—something not easily attainable but full of rewards for those who make the commitment to reach its peak. Latvian literature and folklore also speak of the 'castle of light' as a metaphor for wisdom that has been lost, but will rise again from the depths of the Daugava River after the Latvian people have overcome the intellectual darkness of war, invasion and occupation.

The Archives of Latvian Folklore has been situated within this glass mountain, and it is bustling with activity as its researchers—many young scholars—are devising and following interesting research projects, some of which also relate to the materials gathered during the Soviet period. I asked Baiba Krogzeme-Mosgorda whether these materials were still valuable and how? She told me how Latvian researchers put forth their best efforts to continue with scientific collections and grow the strong tradition of folklore research history in Latvia. At the level of collection they remained largely free to document, although there were instructions not to document anti-Soviet materials and insistence on the collection of "new socialist folklore, like songs about Stalin. These songs obviously did not exist, but soon there emerged composers who were willing to compose songs about Stalin and add them to the materials collected by researchers."

As with the study of folklore in the university, there was another aspect to the activity of collection—the chance to connect with one's own language and culture, even nation, through engagement with folklore. It was a kind of subversive political action.

The Expeditions: The Lithuanian Experience

In Lithuania, where the resistance movement had been the strongest, but crushed, expeditions to collect folklore came up as another opportunity for "nationalism." Lina Būgienė writes about it:

[S]ince the 1960s another dimension became increasingly visible, namely: folklore collection as an organised or individual patriotic activity aimed at opposing the official cultural policy of the Communist Party. Along with individual folklore collectors, the so-called folklore expeditions (i.e. large-scale fieldwork sessions), organised by researchers of the Institute of Lithuanian Language and Literature, higher education teachers, and the Society of Regional Studies (Kraštotyros draugija, see Seliukaitė 1999) rapidly gained momentum during the late 1960s (Sauka 2011, 178). The first such massive fieldwork session was initiated by folklore researcher Norbertas Vėlius in 1963: many young people went to Zervynos collecting folklore—it is a picturesque archaic village in the southern Lithuania. (2017, 30)

While the expeditions were permitted and being supported by the state, the scholars cleverly chose to organize expeditions to the regions where the mass-scale deportations had taken place in the 1940s. The expeditions became a way of connecting with people and sharing a kind of national consciousness. "The political historian and sociologist Ainė Ramonaitė calls this wide informal network of groups and active individuals the "ethno-cultural subculture" of the Soviet times" (31). The ethnocultural aspect was also reflected in the scholars' preference for the collection of pre-Christian folklore, which was seen as more "Lithuanian" than the culture influenced by Christian religion brought in by former colonizers. Ironically, this preference coincided with Soviet authorities' aversion to anything religious and got their support (32). The cooperation with the state by the folklorists or the support of the state to the folklorists was carefully negotiated. Folklore research was done in a situation of uneasy calm.

And [the] second thing was that Russians decided that folklore was a matter of ideological importance of course, and so there was the idea of looking for proletarian folklore [laughs]. . . . And pro-Soviet folklore and it had to be found. I hear all kinds of stories from elderly colleagues as to how this was [laughs] achieved. They had to just invent this folklore; it wasn't there. You had to find songs that glorify Stalin and such ones, whether they were or not. You had to create them. Afterwards appeared folksingers who could create them and were very well valued. On the other hand you could not collect real folklore, which was there: the partisan songs, the resistance fighters there in the forest, they created their own folklore, huge lot of folksongs, romances, which are now published extensively. They were not to be recorded; it was prohibited; they couldn't exist—according to the Soviet understanding. Political jokes [chuckles] ... Never! You could end up in jail if you tried to collect them. Songs of the deportees, people in Siberia; huge part of the population—they also created their own folklore—it was never to be mentioned, it could not be collected and stored in the Archives. And nothing glorifying former bourgeois Lithuanian state.

Anyhow, the expeditions led to a major increase in the holdings of the Folklore Archives in Lithuania. By one account, this increase was of 725,000 folklore texts (31).

In spite of all the careful planning, folklorists could not escape the surveillance by the state and its instrument, the KGB. "After the folklore collectors ventured into Gervėčiai, the part of Belarus that was at the time inhabited mostly by Lithuanians, the folklore expeditions hitherto organized under the aegis of the Society of Regional Studies were banned in 1973, and their leaders had to suffer the consequences" (Būgienė 2017, 32). And yet again, the Lithuanians found another new way of engaging with their culture: "[T]he activity of folklore collection was quickly picked up and promoted further by the Vilnius University students who established the Folklore Club Ramuva [...], by various folk singing groups, by the student hiking groups [žygeiviai], and other informal or semi-formal social networks, mostly uniting young people" (32). As Lina Būgienė told me in 2016, in Lithuania,

These expeditions were stopped. Maybe they [the authorities] sensed that it was getting too national and uncontrollable. Or maybe it was stopped because Vėlius and several others went to Siberia. There were these deportees' villages where Lithuanians were living there. It was several villages ... I don't remember which region it was ... [tries some names]. Never mind, it was Lithuanians living there since nineteenth century when Tsarist regime already exiled some participants of the rebellions. So there were Lithuanians living there already. These folklorists went to collect folklore and language there. Maybe it was a misstep. Some also went to Belorussia where Lithuanians were living by the border and tried to collect folklore there. Russian authorities didn't like that [laughs]. So Russians . . . Soviets decided that it was too out of control. So expeditions were banned, cut down, but this idea was already there, and some organizations tried to organize events like folk-singing programs.

Like Krogzeme-Mosgorda, Būgienė agreed that the materials collected during the expeditions have a lasting value: "It is very good. Really. It's very, very good. It was rather professional. It's very exhaustive. It was based more or less knowing what they were doing. Of course, they could not collect all the folklore. Some part of folklore, some genres were (laughs) out of reach. You couldn't do that. You just didn't report them if you happened to get them, but if people started telling you political jokes you simply couldn't put them into these collections. If they put it, it would be removed (laughs). But anyway as an initiative, as an idea, it was very, very good." These expeditions seem better from today's perspective in yet another respect. In the words of Risto Järv, archivist of the Estonian Folklore Archives,

> [A]fter independence, collection became little problematic . . . Funding became project based . . . Nowadays different projects for archiving, digitizing, research. . . . In Soviet times, there was some continuity . . . It was important. That [expedition] is one good practice from that time . . . It was concentrated on different parts of Estonia . . . because older collections did not have enough from everywhere; so the archivists proposed materials from one area in one year and another area in another year for collection . . . Also, people from other fields of studies joined… so they collected huge mass of materials . . . It was not project based as nowadays . . . No field work expeditions now for [the] last fifteen years because we have no funding . . . So only if someone in

university is interested ... we make short two-week expeditions in
rural area[s] to find if there were storytellers ... In Soviet time[s],
ten or more people went to one place and different genres of folklore
collected from which came different publications.

The same opinion was expressed by many other researchers in all
three countries.

Apart from the support of the state for collection of folklore,
very important factors here are the zeal and commitment of the
Baltic folklorists who worked in these expeditions. In spite of being
aware of the limitations, being sensitive to the repressive nature of
the state they were living in, they put in their best efforts to collect,
compile, and archive the materials. Their commitment should not
be taken for granted as the situation was not very encouraging. As
has been noted in the case of Lithuania, the spread of national consciousness through cultural projects was effective in creating the
peaceful revolt that led to the downfall of Soviet rule. We shall see
the developments that have taken place in all three countries later
in this book, but it is noteworthy here that the work of folklorists
was part of the resistance movement.

I wondered about the influence of the state of terror on the people
and their folklore practices? Did they realize or have the need to strat-
egize while narrating or singing for documentation? The response to
this question came most sharply from Lina Būgienė of the Lithuanian Folklore Archives in Vilnius. "People stopped singing," she told
me. Why? "Because of the repressions—the deportations to Siberia,
which had been so extensive in Lithuania that one-third of the populace was deported, leaving no family untouched." Disruption of continuity was the hallmark of the Soviet rule.

Folklore as national resistance was exactly what Jaago's professor
was practicing and what she calls "parallel knowledge." The complexity inherent in the term "folklore" seems to have been fully in
action during the Soviet occupation of the Baltics. The state is compelled, for its own ideological reasons, to support and fund folklore

research, but the researchers and teachers can subvert the agenda of the state and create an antiestablishment awareness through folklore. Expeditions happened in Lithuania too, the country where resistance to Soviet rule had been the most pronounced and where the terror of deportations had been most widespread.

We cannot miss the repressive nature of the state in this story. The state is not interested in funding a study of people and their lore, but in projecting its own idea of the people through folklore study. In Lithuania, the lines of resistance were more sharply drawn, as mentioned earlier, and therefore supervision and control of folklore too was perhaps stronger.

The Expeditions: The Estonian Experience

In Estonia, as mentioned earlier, the director of the archives, Oskar Loorits, escaped to Sweden just before the arrival of the USSR, and the archives were henceforth censored. Risto Järv of the Estonian Folklore Archives told me that "materials censored were not destroyed but remained in different place, so luckily we can see what was the censoring process. So they [Russians] wanted to continue folklore work but to change the old conceptions. . . . not to have folklore collected by people who left Estonia, not some part of folklore, and third part was that archive should collect and publish new kind of folklore, that is useful to the Soviet regime. So, we had to look for new kinds of materials like, socialistic proverbs." Expeditions took place in Estonia too, and many materials were gathered.

The Legacy

I was struck with the political astuteness and scholarly humility of the Baltic folklorists. Their current achievements are not born out of the USSR times, and much disruption of their institutions and intellectual continuity was caused by the USSR, yet they are able to place matters in a balanced perspective and talk about the single good aspect of the Soviet period for folklore research, namely, the expeditions, which allowed for the continuity of collections, at least. It is clear from all the accounts that the researchers left no stone unturned to utilize this opportunity to the fullest and collect as much and as well as they could. They were not daunted by all the restrictions imposed upon them, but energized by the possibility to collect. And this genuine effort under all odds is what has today become the wealth of folklore in the archives of the Baltic countries.

CHAPTER SIX

RESISTANCE SITE 3
The Countryside

The question here is, What about the third dimension of this drama? Now that we have seen what was happening on stage and behind the curtains, we need to ask where this drama was being performed.

All around the folklore materials and scholars are the subjects of research, that is, the people whose lore was being collected and taught; the people who made the subject of folklore important; the people to whom collectors had gone since the nineteenth century and continued to do so. What was the situation of the folk or the Baltic people in the second half of the twentieth century when the archives had been sanitized, universities supervised, and state-sanctioned academic expeditions being sent to rural areas to collect folklore?

This history of folkloristics remains incomplete without understanding the historical situation of the "folk." From the previous chapters, one can see the differences in the lives of scholars and scholarly institutions. These were obviously only parts of the overall changes in society. One can also sense that the common people were going through even more rigorous repression and changes to their lives. Folklore study and collection were happening amidst all this. One can see that changes were being made in the theoretical framework and institutional functioning by the state very actively with the aim of changing the social and cultural life of the people.

It is evident that the engagement of the folklore scholars in these changes was not voluntary, but it was born out of fear of repression in the first phase and then the evolution of a strategic practice in which one hoped to achieve something minimal. If this was the situation of the scholars, it becomes imperative to reflect on the question regarding the situation of the folk. In more peaceful times, we may concentrate on theoretical folkloristics alone, but the times that are reflected in the treatment of the archives by the state, in the escape of scholars to other countries, in the creation of "parallel worlds" and search for new folklore let one sense that Baltic countries and peoples were going through very unusual and dramatic times. As a foreigner and researcher, I became full of questions about the life in general under the Soviet times, about the countryside and the life of peasantry which was still the source of folklore for the expeditions. Knowledge about the Baltic peoples is indeed limited on an international scale. "The history of the Baltic States is not well known outside of the region itself. This holds true for the period of the Second World War and its aftermath, when the peoples of Lithuania, Latvia, and Estonia suffered multiple occupations, mass killing, large-scale deportations, and radical social transformation, resulting in multiple layers of trauma" (Davoliute and Balkelis 2012, 7).

Siberia in Baltic History

I first became aware of a very important and decisive factor of people's lives in the Baltic countries through the Soviet period in a conversation with Lina Būgienė in 2016. She introduced me to the subject of deportations as the most important form of repression of people by the USSR. She told me:

> My mother was exiled to Siberia with her parents and her sisters
> when she was 3 year old at that time. She was born 1945, and they were

deported to Siberia in 1948. And she spent several years of her youth in Siberia, and she used to tell me stories about how they used to live there. So I knew from my mother's stories what it actually was. [...] Of course, it was very difficult. Another nasty thing was that these deportees, they would take them to the trains in say in May, and they were traveling across big Russia for months, for weeks. When they arrived in Siberia, it was like autumn there, and they were left to ... nothing, to survive the winter. So the first winters were very, very difficult. My mother nearly died. If it wasn't for a local Borage [?] man who fed her [...] mare's milk, she would have died [...]. She was a kid, three years old, and was on the verge of dying. Then they planted some potatoes, and you had huge baskets of it.

Surprised, I asked, "In Siberia?" and Būgienė said, "Yes. The land is very fertile, very good. And if you put something, it grows. But they were not allowed to do that because they were placed there just before the winter. So, winter was the issue to survive, the first winter. Later, it was possible to survive." This conversation was the beginning of a major theme in my study of the history of Baltic folkloristics: mass deportations to Siberia in the postwar period.

Yet another theme that Būgienė introduced was that of growing up during the Soviet period. Būgienė was born at a time when Soviet rule was well established, and people had learned to survive under it. The children had to become part of the ideological system very early in life as they had to join the networks meant for pupils of different ages. She said that "there were three [networks]. When you were seven years old, you had to join Oktobereita—well, it was in Russian: Organization of Little October, because October was the month when Soviet revolution happened, 1917. Then you swiftly joined the Pioneers organization—those red scarves on your neck [laughs], and then you joined the Komsamol—it was the Youth Organization. So it started at the age of seven—the brainwashing, so to say." So, while she was growing up listening to her mother's stories, she "was forced to become a 'pioneer' at school. I became a member of Komsamol, because I could not go to the university if I was not in the Komsamol. It was out of the question."

One can again see the existence of the two-worlds of Jaago, and now not in the dissemination of knowledge at the university, but as the very condition of being. Lina's mother and grandparents were exiled because Lina's uncle had become a resistance fighter and taken to the forests. For this, the entire family was punished for more than a decade of hard life in Siberia. Each deportation to Siberia is a period made of hundreds of small narratives: what happened during the travel; what happened on landing after being carted through various means of transport in an unknown wilderness; how one saw death all around and tried to survive; and if one was not only lucky enough to survive, but also to return to one's homeland, then, what was the life henceforth of self and progeny. I believe these experiences were made across the Baltic countries, as the statistics cited earlier show that people were deported to Siberia from all three countries. For those born in more peaceful times, the stories continued to play an important role. So, while Būgienė continued to join the required networks through her school life, the stories acted as a defense against the propaganda. She said, "I went through all those stages. It was proper upbringing in a way, but it never really touched me deeply in a way that I would become ideologically minded, because I had a very difficult and a very different experience at home, in my family."

It is important to know that this is the story about mass deportations and not about individual repressions that continued throughout the Soviet rule. The USSR deported Baltic people to Siberia en masse first in 1941 and then repeatedly between 1948 and 1953. It is also important to remember that there are three phases in which these experiences can now be conceptualized: first is the phase of mass deportations that lasted until Stalin's death in 1953; second is the phase when deportees who survived the ordeal started returning, beginning in late 1950s; and third is the phase when the Soviet system seemed settled and people compliant, beginning in late 1970s. The third phase was particularly layered, and what seemed calm on the surface was hiding much turbulence underneath. The stories about deportations and life in Siberia and within the Baltic countries started bursting forth from the moment the USSR began to collapse, in 1990, and the narration continues.

As it was not possible to publicly give expression to these experiences under the Soviet rule, except in hushed tones within close family circles, the open verbalization is in the form of memory. Therefore, memory as a factor of consideration and memory studies are closely linked to the study of the expressions of experiences of the deportees which have appeared as autobiographies, as answers to interview questions, and as "life stories" written by common people in response to calls by the Estonian Cultural Archive. Generation and collection of life stories have followed different methods (as we shall discuss later) and have been initiated by different disciplines, notably ethnology, sociology, history, and cultural studies. These life stories can be studied and analyzed to gain a view of the life outside the folklore archives and university departments during the Soviet period. In this chapter, the life stories are presented to show the larger context in which the study of folklore was evolving in the Baltic countries during the Soviet period. I am not aware that this connection has been established before in writing about Baltic folkloristics.

Quite recently, narratives concerning family history remained in the intermediate area between disciplines. In the period when the walls between fields of science were relatively inflexible because of specialisation, these narratives were too poetic for historians and the data in the narratives could not be used because they were not as reliable as church registers, inspection reports and other traditional historical sources. For folklorists these stories were too information-centred, factual. These narratives lacked the characteristic features of folklore. (Jaago https://lepo.it.da.ut.ee/~lehti/Oralhistory/3.9.Tiiu.htm)

In the following, we shall see that these narratives are influenced by the genres of folklore, and narrators make direct and indirect references to them. Yet, they are not the "traditional" folklore materials and are not treated here as folklore, but as oral history.

Gathering Siberian Experience in Estonia

In Estonia, the first active round of collection of "life stories" happened between 1989 and 1991. The first call remained open until 1997, and fresh calls were issued in 1995, 1996, 1997, 1998, and 1999. Each call differed thematically, but they were all about life during the Soviet period. This has been one of the most organized attempts at gathering information, narratives, and histories for which no other records exist. Even the exact number of deportees cannot be ascertained owing to the obvious difficulties (whether USSR kept the records, and whether they will ever show these to anyone). In this context, the projects to gather life stories gain immense significance. Järv, told me that the last two projects were called "My Homeland" and "My Landscape." So, the efforts to document, understand, analyze, and publish the history of people's lives during the Soviet period are very much on in Estonia and are also picking up pace in Latvia and Lithuania.

As should be self-evident, the life stories were written by people in their own language, that is, Estonian. Therefore, even if the archives were to make them all public, a researcher like me will not be able to read them. However, a set of stories, by both men and women, has been translated and published separately. I base my thoughts and understanding of the life of the "folk" in Estonia under the Soviet rule on these stories, my conversations with ethnologists Tiiu Jaago and Kristin Kuutma, archivist Risto Järv, and historian Aigi Rahi-Tamm, as well as my reading of published ethnological and history works.

"I am old now, but when I think back upon my life, it is hard to believe that it was my life and it was I, who experienced it!" (Kirss, Kõresaar, and Lauristin 2004, 226). So starts the life story of Aino, a woman who was the teenaged daughter of a locomotive engine driver in 1941, when she became one of the thousands of Estonians deported to Siberia on the night of June 14, 1941. What followed was not only a diversion from the expected future of a middle-class girl of an educated family, but the beginning of a life of unimaginable hardships that would bring out her character in unexpected ways. Once in Siberia, she worked in a *kolkhoz* (a collective farm) in 1942. As one of her jobs, she was asked to float logs down the stream, for which she received four hundred grams of peas as a daily wage (227). She was then transferred to several other places where she received meager rations for very hard work in temperatures below -35 degrees celsius. This was the Soviet Union's idea of equality of men and women, that is, hard labor for women (227–29). Extreme sickness followed (230), from which she nearly died. And here her individual character started asserting itself. She escaped in 1946 (232). Escaping from Siberia was not a joke. First, the terrain and the climate themselves were great hindrances. Second, the entire area and the deportees were kept under surveillance, and punishments for escape were severe enough to deter most people from attempting to escape from their tormentors. Aino's account of escape is thus long and cannot be reproduced here in its entirety, but it is full of extraordinary bravery, immense bodily hardships, and mental resilience. She had left Siberia on December 14, 1946, and reached Estonia on February 24, 1947 (232–35). Her relatives were surprised at her return, but they took care of her and brought her back to some form of health. It is important to mention here that in Estonia there was extreme rationing at the time, and feeding one more mouth than officially registered meant partial hunger for others. However, she was able to make a passport and have a job, but she was interrogated by the KGB (236). She managed to convince them that she was just another Estonian and not a runaway from Siberia. She also got married. And then the KGB found out about her.

She was pregnant when she was arrested in 1950, imprisoned, and sent to Siberia again (237). As punishment, she was given a thirty-year sentence (239). Subsequently, her husband was also arrested as political prisoner and sent to another location in Siberia (238–39). Aino continued to do hard labor in Siberia, paying the state (after World War II, the USSR was in a terrible economic condition).

After Stalin's death in 1953, such workers did not have to pay the state anymore and started getting their wages. "At the end of 1955 I was given 2 tons of wheat for two years of work, 700 kgs of oats, 2 buckets of honey and as a premium 8000 rubles in actual cash." With part of all this wealth, she bribed officials to get permission to visit her husband in a coal mining camp (239).

What a meeting! Aino's portrayal of a jail-like coal-mine camp on a bleak winter day is picturesque and evidently stored as such in her memory. There was a room for such couples to meet in for the allotted hours. While she waited there for her husband to be brought, the guards and other officials made lurid comments (240). What could such a meeting be but sad and hopeless and yet so important for them as a reason to go on living. She returned to continue to live and hope. After some time, her husband was released, and joined her. In 1958 they and their children were released and returned to Estonia (241), although they were not permitted to go back to the region of their birth. They rebuilt their lives. Aino ends her narrative: "This then is the story of one simple, ordinary Estonian woman among thousands who were deported to Siberia. That is all: just hard work, great tribulation and finally heaven!" (241). In these last words, a folklorist cannot miss the entire trope of the folk tale: hardships, test-by-fire and/but a happy ending!

One gets a really wide canvas of life from women's perspectives in the three stories of women connected as mother-daughter-grand-daughter, with the daughter writing the story of the mother and her own. This canvas shows life from 1865 to 1990. The mother,

Siliima Mann was born in 1865 on a large farm and married young into a family with a large farm (264). The life on large farms was comfortable but involved the hard work of all the family members. Siliima Mann can be said to have lived an Estonian life, which was a reality of some and dream of many more. She had farm, family, and children, a faith to depend on, and continuity of tradition until she was old. She became a widow in 1928. In 1944, when the world around her started to change drastically, she had a son in the Estonian army who was automatically drafted into the Soviet army (265). Soon after, her farm was taken away from private possession and became a *kolkhoz* (266). In spite of such submission to the new state of things, at the age of 84, in 1949, she was deported to Siberia for being "an enemy of the people"—a term applied in the USSR to anyone who was not exactly poor. She was deported along with her sixty-three-year-old daughter. Mann survived the hardships and made it to Siberia but died in 1955, two weeks before her ninetieth birthday (267). Mann was only one of many elderly people who were deported.

Mann's story was narrated by Helmes, her fourteenth child, born in 1907. Helmes became a school teacher in 1930, a significant achievement for women of her generation. She was the director of the village school when the Soviets occupied Estonia and deportations started. When her mother and sister were deported in 1949, Helmes was forced to resign from her job and give up her farms. She had married in 1944, and her husband was in the Estonian army. He had been discharged in 1945 and had become a teacher in the same school (271). Her daughter Leelo was born in 1947. Helmes was deported in 1950 and was imprisoned for months in Patarei prison, Tallinn (272), which was infamous as a torture camp. She was then sentenced and sent to Siberia to a life of hard labor in coal mines. She learned to survive, and after a few years, some mail contact with family members was permitted. She was released in 1955, after Stalin's death, and returned to Estonia where she was reunited with her daughter and husband (273–74). "I cannot describe my feeling at such a reunion. I was back home as in a fairy tale, and the nightmare receded into the past" (275)—this is how she remembered it. She was lucky and even got back her job at the school in Ruila, although its nature with reference to daily terms and conditions of education had changed. However, like almost the entire population, she had been sufficiently terrorized into submission. She would not only never raise her head against authority, but she would be enthusiastic about her daughter doing all the ideal things that a child in the Soviet school system was expected to do, as becomes evident in her daughter Leelo's story.

Leelo calls her life story "extraordinarily typical," signifying the fact that it represents the story of many others born during the Soviet period. Born in 1947, she was secretly baptized at home (276). She started having horrible nightmares in March 1949 (277). Although she did not make the connection explicit, this was after the deportation of her grandmother and grandaunt perhaps, because she remembers her grandaunt's deportation (278). Then, in 1950, her mother did not come back home, as she—Helmes— was deported. Leelo says, "Waiting for Memme's return was a very long torment." Her father and aunts took care of her, but she continued to ask for and about her mother. In a heavenly turn of events, her mother returned, and then started Leelo's own life (279–82).

She was an enthusiastic and participative child at school, which meant being part of children's organizations promoted by the state, wearing the prescribed scarf and waving the flag of the USSR (283). Such was her enthusiasm, supported by her parents, that she was selected to go for a camp in Moscow at the age of thirteen (285). With much excitement and fanfare, she was seen off by the family. Once at the camp, however, she innocently and instinctively did things that turned the tide against her. And what a tide it was! She became a black sheep for going on a walk by herself and for not eating vinaigrette in the cafeteria. Even when forced to eat, she could not, and when she fainted due to not eating and perhaps the stress, she was identified "a vintage enemy of the people." Consequently, she was sent to the infirmary, called the "isolator." During one of the later events, she was about to win a table tennis match and find acceptance again, but the male coach announced that her "serves had a Japanese spin which were not allowed in 'our country' and which required my disqualification." At the end of the camp, all kids were given medals, diplomas, books, and so on, but not Leelo, as she had been "a bad one" (286–87). She returned home thin and dispirited, much to the shock and surprise of her family. Thus, she remained largely uninterested for the rest of her time in school. The state itself had finished her naïve enthusiasm. Later, she studied philology at the University of Tartu and led a bohemian life. Life, loves, marriages, also a return as teacher in the Ruila school made up the trajectory of her life under the Soviet system (290–96). Why did she want to narrate her life story? This is a question she perhaps asked herself and answered in the last sentence of her narrative: "This work is dedicated not only to the victims of fascism and communism, but to those honest people who could not survive the terrorism of selfish profit and brutality, even in peacetime" (287–98). Indeed, Leelo grew up in the so-called peace times, and yet she has much to be sad about. Life under the Soviet rule was not peaceful even in "peaceful" times.

The stories of Siliima, Helmes, and Leelo cover a period of more than 125 years. Siliima's life remains an image of what many would believe to be the Estonian way of life before World War II changed the "homeland" of the Estonian peoples. This image is of life in the countryside, of large families, of hard work, of faith, and of patriotism. While many foreign rulers had come and gone, and while life had changed over the past centuries as well, it was defined by continuity. The USSR came and broke that asunder. It brutalized not only people but also the landscape and destroyed agricultural knowledge and practices that had evolved over centuries. The extent of the destruction is such that reconnecting after 1990 becomes yet another question to explore. We shall return to it in due course.

Before that, however, let us consider the life stories of two more women: one was trapped between the three forces of independent

Baltic states between world wars, Germans, and Russians; and the second was not deported to Siberia but was sent to Estonia from Russia. The first story, that of Minna, deals with the question of what it meant to have been politically active as a nationalist or Communist between the two world wars, that is, when Balts were living in independent nations. The second story, that of Elmine, represents a minority group—the ethnic Estonians living in Russia since long before the wars. Elmine's story is simultaneous to, and yet the opposite of, the Estonian women's story in many ways. It also shows that some did have very different experiences in the USSR.

Minna was a young girl who fell in love with a school teacher who arrived from town in the village between the two world wars. Young, educated, and a violin player—the man stole her heart for she too came from an educated family with a love of music. But this school teacher brought new kinds of songs to the village—songs about the future, about hope in the change of worldly order, and about a time when human relations would be redefined. Soon he told her that he was a Communist. She was alarmed, wanted to move away from him, because she thought this was against her belief in God. But she could not move away nor give up her religious ceremonies altogether. Soon they were married (299–300). Then, in 1940, Communists came to the country and then to the village. The man became in charge of important affairs. They moved to town and had a child. In 1941, Nazis came. They left the child at home and agreed that he would go away without telling her where so that she did not have to reveal it when questioned. Very soon after his leaving, soldiers knocked at her door, asked her about him, and then arrested her. She was put in a lorry by the Germans and taken to a concentration camp in Germany. There were one hundred thousand people in this camp. So, before their turn to be gassed came, there were many other deaths to be endured. And Minna, along with many other Russian girls, had to do the menial tasks required. She lived in inhuman living conditions. It was extremely cold, and hard labor was required of her. She was often abused for being a

Russian Communist. In a way, she too waited for death (305–06). In 1943, Russians came as victors of the war and took over everything. Now she was again an enemy—a Nazi employee of the concentration camp (307). She again suffered hard labor and abuse until a Russian officer took a fancy to her and started meeting her in the evenings. They married while he was posted in Germany (308–09). They moved to Russia, his homeland, where she was a foreigner, with a child and did not understand the language of her new family (310). Then he got a posting in Estonia, and they left Germany. She tried to trace her family, her daughter, whom she did not recognize and who took a long time to call her "mother." She had a comfortable life with her Russian husband and children in Soviet Estonia. At the age of seventy, however, when she had been a widow for many years, she lost one of her two sons in an accident, which left her a broken person once again.

Minna's story shows the crazy situation that Estonian society experienced as a whole: at a time, in the 1920s and 1930s, when they were building their first independent state, they were caught between the opposing forces of Communist Russians and Nazi Germans. If they were nationalists, they were persecuted by the Russians. If they were Communists, they were persecuted by the Germans. If they had been politically aloof and cooperated with whomever was in power, they were persecuted by both. It seems to have been impossible to escape violence and torture.

This is the life story of Elmine, born in 1918 in Russia, to parents living in abject poverty. They were ethnic Estonians whose ancestors had migrated east in the nineteenth century, when Estonia was under the rule of Tsarist Russia. Such migration and diaspora populace from the Baltic countries in the USSR were known minorities. Elmine's life has been such that she asks in the beginning of her life story, "How to begin my life story?" She answers, "Probably from my parents who gave me life" (318). Indeed, there wasn't much else parents could give. From a poor, landless family trying to survive somehow in postrevolution Russia, the family was shifted around and put to work in some *kolkhoz*. Elmine went to an Estonian-lan-guage school in Merjovo, but it was closed down when all things Estonian were banned. This was probably the result of Estonia being occupied by Germany in 1941 and collaborating with Germany, a fact not known to her in those years. She considers, "The years 1937–38 were tragic for many good people." However, she completed her basic education and got a job. She narrated life in Communist Russia from a worker's perspective: "The Russians worked without enthusiasm. No one cared how things turned out. Everything was slip-shod. Of course we received no wages. Our family barely sub-sisted." Her father ultimately became a tractor driver by learning on the job in 1940 in Luuga and trained her in 1941 (319). She was sent to Leningrad in 1944 where women were doing all jobs like "driving tractors, being cutters, locksmiths" and men were sent "as bayonets" to battlefields and "were dying like flies" (320).

As the war ended and the USSR took control of the Baltic coun-tries, several Communist activists were sent to live there so as to play the role of when there were hardly any natives to fulfill the role. Along with Communists, ethnic Balts were encouraged to go as the state thought they would be better to spread the propaganda. So, soon after the war, Elmine too was called to the Communist Party office and asked if she wanted to go to Estonia. "I knew noth-ing about Estonia and had almost forgotten the language. I could not even imagine a country where everyone spoke Estonian. Used to living in communal dwellings, the term 'home' meant nothing to me. Wherever I lived was home. I accepted the offer. Anything new and interesting appealed to me" (320). With such disenchant-ment in her twenties, Elmine arrived in Estonia to find no one in the Communist Party office waiting for her. She spent the first days feeling lost, but then found some party workers. She looked around for work and got sundry small jobs. In the course of time, she sent letters to the Communist Party asking for them to allow her mother, father, and brother to join her. They came too. She also got the good news that her other sisters were also alive in Estonia, near Viljandi.

Her sisters had been brought to Estonia by Germans in cattle carts and hired as servants by farmers. When Russians regained control over Estonia, keeping servants was banned. So the eldest son of one farmer asked one of the sisters to marry him. She did and remained there for life. The other sister went to work at a post office. All sisters had a reunion in the summer of 1946 at the farm—and that was the first true holiday for them all (321).

In 1948, Elmine got a tractor driver's job and says of that moment "that my real life had finally begun." For the local Estonians, it was the time of censorships, repressions, and deportations, while Elmine was hardly aware of it. For her, Estonia was a foreign country, still very different from the Communist Russia she had known. Elmine loved her job out in nature. One Sunday she saw a group of people outside a church with girls in white dresses and found them "like apparitions" and looked at herself in work overalls with parched skin and cracked hands—"A sudden weariness overcame me, when I realized that I did not even look like a woman!" (323). The scene also speaks of her isolation and distance from the local Estonians. She had indeed not returned to her "homeland" as connections had been severed for generations. She was neither Russian nor Estonian. In 1949 she witnessed the destruction of Estonian farms and farmers and their deportation to Siberia but had no way of understanding it in any other manner except as explained by the state in its propaganda.

However, her own life was evolving at another plane. She was trained further as a combine harvester operator. She became famous as the only female operator. In 1950, she was invited to Tallinn for the celebration of the liberation of Estonia and awarded the Order of Lenin (324). She was the perfect material to be shaped into the image of a worker that the USSR wanted to portray. In 1951, she was also made district party nominee and was told that she would be representing Soviet power and given one thousand rubles to buy new clothes. Then she was back to her tractor work in one of the new *kolkhoz* farms in Estonia. Again, she was sent to Moscow for a conference where she presented the idea of forming an Estonian Women's Tractor Operators' Brigade. Her idea was accepted, and she became the symbol of workers' power. She experienced the grandiose Moscow and inspiring leaders (325). In 1952, she formed the brigade in Estonia.

Elmine married a man similar in profile and portrayed her union as that of "four able hands and two loving hearts" (326). She began a domestic life that was completely different from that of her parents. She had a child in 1953 and in the same year went to the International Women's Congress in Denmark, a rare privilege in the USSR. This shows how much she was trusted by the state that she could be sent to a Western country. At the time, her husband was under compulsory military training and her child at home. Yet, she could have run away. Of course, the thought never entered Elmine's head. In 1958, she was awarded the highest honors—Order of Lenin and Heroic Socialist Workers' Gold Star. That was what she calls "[the] golden year of my life." She had truly moved on in life. In the same year, the tractor depot was disbanded as the new combine machine came in. Her family remained near Viljandi where they built a house (327). But Elmine had yet to achieve many new heights. In 1969, she spoke at the Kolkhoz Workers Congress in Moscow in the Kremlin's Congressional Palace. In 1974, she received a call telling her that a combine had arrived in her name and went to see a bright orange combine with the words "For the heroic Socialist Worker E. P. Otsman from the Rostrelmas Factory Collective" printed on it. This was honor at its best—a worker celebrated by other workers! In 1973, she and many other soviet women received a bronze Pasha bust. In 1983, her son Aivar became a harvester, and thus the family tradition was already in its third generation (328).

Then the USSR collapsed. Where did that leave Elmine? She realized the flaws in the *kolkhoz* system and said they were never really united. And although she never knew the Estonian Free Republic of the interwar years or its flag colors, she was happy at independence in 1991. One would think that she would recall her experience of the USSR as a positive one. Yet, although she was proud of what she did and was able to narrate those moments of achievement with her level of knowledge and state of being at that time, her realizations were more than she reveals. She says,

> It seems that my life was spent in a period of great deceit, and because of that all my life's ideals have been shattered. They cannot be put back together. [. . .] Faith, religious holidays and Christmas had not entered my life until recently. If only I could believe that God exists! I was born, grew up and worked under the Soviet system. When I arrived in Estonia the system was the same. How was I to know that it had been quite different, that this small nation was occupied? [. . .] Having seen the destruction of the farms and the result, I have now experienced the exact opposite—the breaking up of the collectives, the redistribution of land and efforts to re-establish private family hold-ings. My dear gentlemen in the city, you cannot do this with farmland. It took many years to build the kolkhoz system and now you want to reverse it in one year! [. . .] And where are our true farmers—the ones with the know-how? This does not happen overnight. The skills, the traditions have been lost. Only time can re-build what has been lost. (329–30)

She ends by wishing to see Estonia as the most honest land where everyone feels safe and "goodness should reign in the world." Soon after, she questions her own wish: "Is that humanly possible?" and answers in a word, "Hardly!" (330).

Elmine's narrative has another kind of sadness: to become some-body from nobody in the USSR, to experience the system positively and then get connected to the land of your ancestors to realize how she herself was part of the system that destroyed it. In spite of such positive experience, she did not believe that goodness can reign in the world. Was this disenchantment born of the failure of the *kolk-hoz* system or the impossibility of Estonians to be able to return to the pre-Soviet system?

The Estonian Literature and Folklore Archives started by open-
ing the life-stories contest. People were invited to send in their stories. Some eight hundred were received in the very first round, and
by now about three thousand life stories are stored there. Not all
have been worked upon, and very few translated into English. This
material is equally important for historians, ethnologists, anthropologists, and folklorists. It is the only record of a time on which state
records are largely not available or if they are, they cannot be trusted.
Commenting on the life stories in Estonia, Ene Kõresaar, ethnologist
and one of the editors of the volume *She Who Remembers, Survives*
(2004) raises "The Inverse Question: The Collective in the Individual" and tells the readers, "For our research problematic the central
question is the relationship between communicative and cultural
memory, and how this relationship makes itself felt on the level of
individual memory" (40). Elaborating on the subject, she says, "For
life stories researcher who is studying collective memory through
[auto]biographical narrative, the key question is how the 'layers' of
social memory exert an influence on autobiographical memory and
biographical knowledge in a broader sense [. . .], or how the cog-
nitive and interpretive frames influence an individual's perception
of reality and actions." (45). She concludes "Life experiences shape
every individual biography. [. . .] Life experiences and the biographical knowledge that is gained from them create in the biography a
connection between the past and the future. They are resources
which are applied in the formation of future life projects" (46).

Gathering Life under Soviet Rule in Latvia

Life stories have also been collected in Latvia. "The conditions for
developing a collection of life stories and for studying oral history
were set in place by the late 1980s in Latvia, when the country experienced the Atmoda [Reawakening]" (Garda Rozenberga 2012, 257).
The process began at the same as that in Estonia, but the method

has been significantly different from that of the Estonian collectors. In Estonia, people were given a broad theme and asked to send their life stories written by themselves. These texts were thus formulated by the individuals themselves who might have made more than one draft of the text, apart from having the possibility to reflect upon it. As such, its importance is enhanced by the fact that these narratives are what the people wanted to tell about themselves and told without the presence of a researcher. In Latvia, the life stories were recorded on audio, in the late 1980s and early 1990s on tapes and later digitally. The researchers were present and did ask questions, but followed predecided methodological paradigms that we shall detail in this chapter. The importance of their record is that they have people's narratives in their own voices, including the thinking time taken by individuals. One can hear the way someone is constructing the record of life.

In May 2017, I visited the Latvian National Oral History Archives in Riga where I spoke with Ieva Garda Rozenberga, Māra Zirnīte, Edmunds Šūpulis, and Baiba Bela about the process, method, and contents of the life stories recorded in Latvia. While some research articles on the subject have emerged in English, life stories have not yet been translated.

Māra Zirnīte and Ieva Garda Rozenberga told me about their first academic head professor: Augusts Milts, who was a philosopher of ethics. Ieva said, "He studied ethics and philosophy and started oral history in this paradigm—of ethics. We continue his work and style." Augusts Milts's theory of values has been the guiding principle behind the study of the life stories, particularly the life stories of those who escaped Latvia in 1945 to live in other countries (Zirnīte and Garda Rozenberga 2014, 11).

The National Oral History Archives in Riga recorded life stories geographically as well as from all the different communities in Latvia. It was interesting to hear that "Latvia was divided after World War II," referring to many Latvians leaving the country to go live elsewhere. Māra said, "It is important because it is great exodus of

Latvians at the end of World War II in 1945. Many people fly away from Latvia because they were afraid of the returning Red Army. It is the reason why you can meet very many exiled people in Europe countries." Ieva added, "We also want to preserve oral histories as cultural heritage. One special aim is to facilize the unification of the experience of the Latvian nation, which was divided in World War II. So we interview Latvians in US, in Germany, England, Sweden ... in all these countries where they moved as refugees. And they don't know what the experience of Latvians was here in Soviet times, and we didn't know what their lives were in their new countries."

Māra Zirnīte said that there are many different ethnic backgrounds in Latvia:

> Livonians on the western coast, lived from historical time, but separate
> story, will show you a presentation, but current time nobody who
> can speak Livonian, because people went out in Soviet time, it was
> forbidden to work here. They could not go to fish in the sea in Soviet
> times. But it is very interesting, they are related to the Estonians.
> Their language belongs to the Finno-Ugric group. Another diversity
> is on the eastern part—Ladgalians. Inside all Latvia, there are many
> Russian people—it is the main minority as we say. And Jewish, Polish,
> Estonians, and Lithuanians not many, then Roma, Ukrainians, and
> Belorussian.

So, Oral History Archives researchers go to all the regions and to different communities to record life stories. "In the context of globalization, region is significant because of its historical roots and the cultural tradition it contains therein as well as a measure according to which existing norms and social ties are much more secure and provide the individual real support" (Zirnīte 2005, 171). Ethnic variation within Latvia is an important consideration for the Oral History Archives. One of the recently completed projects was Ethnic and Narrative Diversity in Latvia, wherein life stories of Latvians, Russians, and Roma people have been recorded. Edmunds Šūpulis, who was one of the people involved in this research, expressed the importance of comparing the narratives from different communities to understand history:

> At first, of course, Latvians were like a background of these stories. From Russians we heard stories, normally they have roots here from ancient time, but we also know about arrival of many after World War II, and they are completely different stories of attachment to place from those who lived here and those who arrived. The Roma people, not so trained; it's not something usual for them to tell about their life. So we had to overcome some suspicion: who are we? Why are we interested in their life? And then stories came at last, and of course it is huge, huge unknown fields of experiences and how they feel among us, how they manage to survive, and their way of life.

The Romas have lived in Latvia for ages and were quite integrated in the Latvian society, although they carried on with their own way of life in a seminomadic style. During the German occupation in the early part of World War II, they were exterminated en masse, and mainly by the Latvians. This remains a problematic memory for the Latvians and the Romas. It is interesting to see how they fared during the Soviet period. Edmunds Šūpulis said,

> So, in Soviet times, it was a policy of social system that you have to work, you have to have permanent residence, and what was good was that you have to have education. And Roma remember. One woman said it was first time that Roma were perceived as people, as man [...]. It was first time when government was interested in them, how to settle them, give them flats, bring their children to school. And for instance, this memory differs from Latvians'. For Latvians, Soviet army came not as liberators. In our collective memory, they came as occupants, as colonizing forces. But for Roma people, they came as liberators; they were emancipators I'd say, because it was really possibility for children to go to schools, they were provided with jobs, their living

standards raised. Yes. So they have completely different memories and experience of this alien regime, Soviet regime.

The Oral History Archives makes a difference in the understanding of the people of Latvia in important ways, as is evident in the way Šūpulis differentiates between the formerly available knowledge about the Roma and that caused by oral history projects: "There are anthropologists who talked about Roma people. They are presented as people who don't remember, don't care about history, have no such historical narratives as national entities. So it was interesting to talk about their memories."

Varied narratives present a more complex view of history than single narratives. For the majority of Latvians, there are several topics that are of concern. Zirnīte says that "there are several topics about Soviet time. Soviet time began in 1940 but it was war-time. When soviet rule starts after war, then in beginning, it is very difficult for many people because they are not used to such hard rules. Many people disappear; so that's one topic. Second topic is first occupation by Germans, then started occupation by Russians. Then topics of resistance against repression. Then topics about deportation. And this confrontation with power."

These topics also relate to the various generations from whom the stories have been recorded. Baiba Bela said that

it was the middle of [the] nineties. At that moment, the negative things about Soviet times were stressed, the positives were silenced. And also, for example, collaboration with Soviet authorities. For example: being in the Communist Party was silenced. Being in Communist Party was told when there was a good excuse. For example, a lady who had four kids, and her husband was killed, he was a former legionnaire. So he fought in the "wrong" army in World War II. She was a school teacher and was invited to join the Communist Party, and of course her decision was yes, because she did not want to risk to give up her job; she has four kids to raise. But in other cases, about being in the Communist Party, we get to know through other people's stories.

I was naturally interested in how this representation has changed over the last twenty-seven years of independence. Bela responded, saying, "I think the generation has changed. When we interviewed people in nineties, their youth was spent in independent Latvia before war. But those who are interviewed at the present, their whole life, more or less, was in Soviet times. Pre-Soviet time was probably very early childhood. So main life was in Soviet times and you can't tell negative things about your whole life. If something was positive, it is not silenced any more." This change in the expression of memory of Soviet times has been observed in Estonia, too: "[F]rom the denial of Soviet-era experiences/past immediately after the restoration of independence, re-membering has become multi-vocal during the first decade of the 21st century" (Jõesalu, 2017: 69).

The questions is, What was positive during the Soviet period? Baiba was quick to respond: "Social life, social securities. For example, in the countryside, everyone had work. Then at the *kolkhoz* and culture house, they often had parties. For example, excursions, and even visit to theater—it was quite regular that *kolkhoz* took a big bus, everyone got into the bus and came to city for theatre. At present, it is not possible for many country people who don't have car to come to Riga for theater."

As Zirnīte said, it is the special or unique thing about the life story records in Latvia that were recorded on audio tapes. Recording implies the presence of the researcher, so I wanted to know how the interviews were conducted. Ieva said, "We go to people to record interviews. We try not to ask questions, not to bother or interrupt them, but just to listen how they are constructing their life stories; the theme they want to start or finish their life story. After about two or three hours long conversation then we ask some particular questions." Bela said that it also depends on the person being interviewed as some people are more forthcoming than others who require prodding.

The experience of documenting and studying life stories is thus different in Latvia from that in Estonia. The difference is both in the method and in the conclusions. This does not imply contradictions as the narrative of the majority community in Latvia—the Latvians—is similar to that of the Estonians, but the additional narratives of the minority communities make the picture more complex. In documenting varied narratives, the oral history researchers in Latvia also bring forth the complexity in characterizing the Soviet period. On the whole, there are too many similarities across the Baltic countries during the Soviet period: for example, the *kolkhoz* system or the "collective farm" introduced and instituted by the USSR.

An important observation from working with complementary methods of oral history interview, life writing and ethnography was that, when used inter-changeably, different methods make it possible to grasp the dynamics of post-communist remembering step by step and to identify its contested fields. In the second half of the 1990s, while life writing and published memoirs contributed to forming the historical image of a suffering nation, researchers' ethno-graphic notes from the same time reported the evolution of nostalgia as a form of criticism of the post-communist condition. (Kõresaar and Jõesalu 2006, 52)

The Soviet Period in Historical Perspective

Lina Būgienė, who opened the subject of deportations to me in such a manner that I decided to make it a part of the history of folkloristics in the Baltic countries, also talked about the destruction of the countryside and agriculture by the USSR. This destruction was even more severe in Lithuania as the resistance to the USSR was more intense, and farmers were seen as supporting the rebels who used to hide in the forests near the villages. Not only did the *kolkhoz* system not take off; there was hardly any farming for decades. Lina told me, "Farmers could not farm because their tools and animals had been taken away. For decades there was nothing to do in the countryside but sit and try to cultivate some potatoes for survival." This destroyed not only agricultural practices but also agricultural knowledge. Her colleague, the director of the Lithuanian Literature and Folklore Archives said to me, "Villages are dying in Lithuania. One can see abandoned villages all across." Just a little over half a century ago, the Balts were agrarian and pastoral people. The loss of agricultural practices does not just imply what it obviously does, but it also implies snapping ties with one's habitat as a place that can provide for the continuity of life. Could this be one of the reasons why there is currently such heavy migration out of Lithuania?

In Estonia, the *kolkhoz* system took off in some regions, as people were terrorized into submission and had older ways of collaborative farming. The situation was better than in Russia. Kristin Kuutma told me that even peacetime wasn't peacetime because produce from such areas started being sent to Russia because the *kolkhoz* system was a failure there, but Moscow needed everything. Heavy industry was planted across Estonia and Latvia, and Russians were encouraged to move to Estonia to live there and work in these industries. Today Russians are a sizeable minority in all the three Baltic countries, and relationships between the Balts and them are not without conflict. It is understandable that they do not wish to return to Russia, but the life stories clearly show that the Balts have too many painful memories of the Russian rule, and in some ways, they are also important today.

Through conversations with Aigi Rahi-Tamm, an Estonian historian at the University of Tartu, I tried to gain an understanding of how these life stories applied to an understanding of the Soviet period. She added another dimension by saying, "In this history [narrated in life stories], there are the perpetrators and the victims at two ends, but in history there are also the by-standers in between that constituted the majority of the populace." Indeed, what about the "by-standers"? What is their role in this history? They did not suffer directly, but they also formed opinions and passed them on to their progeny. "And then, those who collaborated actively with the Soviet authorities, those who had other Estonians deported for selfish gains or personal animosities, those stories are not out, but people know them," said Rahi-Tamm. So, people also know that being Estonian does not mean belonging to one harmonious whole. In *She Who Remembers Survives* (2004), in her analysis of Aino's life story, Rahi-Tamm discusses such a connection:

> In her new place of residence Aino also meets up with the head of the Tapa militia, who had interrogated her at one time. *I cannot remember that militia head's name anymore, a tall Estonian with curly hair; I have seen him in these parts, he has a summer home near Kohtla-Nomme. He does not recognize me, but I recognize him, a disgusting site.* Aino is one of those sufferers who does not need revenge, though she considers it natural that apologies should be made for what happened. Many of the problems of the recent past have yet to been [*sic*] worked through. Despite conflicted emotions, these harsh decades require systematic analysis. (86) (emphasis in original)

Yet another important aspect of this history—the policy that governed the deportations and other sociocultural issues—is also not under the academic scanner. Rahi-Tamm went on to tell me, "There are the life stories to study, but the policy that governed them cannot be studied because that must be as records in Moscow, Russia, and are not available for study. As a state, Russia has neither acknowledged nor regretted the Deportations."

Our conversation took a detour to folk narratives and their role in such extraordinary times: "The deportees narrated them to their children (who were also deported in large numbers along with parents, and those that were born in Siberia) to tell them about their homeland Estonia. It was on these stories that children's idea of their homeland was built on, the homeland they longed for, and which they aspired to reach." A crucial role indeed—to keep alive the hope and continuity of life and cultural-spatial identity—was thus played by folk narrative in these times, as several times before in history—in Estonia, the Baltics, and elsewhere in the world. Folk narratives have been part of ordinary folks' lives in myriad ways. Life stories collected through calls by archives are also narratives, but they are located in the recent past, and therefore in referable "reality." For scholars, they constitute "oral history"—a field that combines the discipline of history and others like ethnology and folkloristics specializing in the study of orality. Whatever the categorization for the sake of analysis, but what is their role in contemporary history to which they belong? Rahi-Tamm elaborated the complexities in the role that the life stories are playing: "The role of these life stories in today's Estonia is that they influence people's perception about Russia and state's policy towards Russia. Neither the young nor the old want to have anything to do with Russia, nor trust Russians. That influences the way Russian populace of Estonia is viewed too, which is problematic."

"The oral popular history research direction in Estonian folkloristics is the broadest of all the aforementioned. The creation of this direction is connected with the rethinking of the whole of folkloristics from the starting point of the communicativeness of texts," writes Rutt Hinrikus, the initiator of the documentation of life stories and one of the three editors of the volume *She Who Remembers, Survives,* which contains the translated life stories. The life-stories project is a collaborative project among historians, ethnologists, and folklorists in Estonia.

History and Folklore

For me, the importance of these narratives for the study of the history of folkloristics in Estonia during the Soviet period is to understand the broader social context in which folklore research and institutions of its study were functioning and evolving. What emerges is stunning—that in a period of such extreme collective stress, folklore institutions and scholars maintained continuity and carried on with folklore research. Although the state did not dismantle the folklore discipline, the kind of hurdles it placed in its path are no small matter. What the archives went through, what the researchers there were required to do, what the teachers in the University had to comply with, what the students and teachers could or could not verbalize and yet communicated with each other— these are experiences that are also subjects of life stories of people connected with the study of folklore. After reading the life stories, of which I have cited only a few, I could not but rethink the "expeditions" on which folklorists went to collect folklore with the permission of the state. The way in which they continued the work started by Jakob Hurt demands respect. But the villages and folk they went to were going through very intense changes or had just been through them and were adjusting to new realities.

The farms they would have visited would have been *kolkhoz*; many owners of those lands would have been sent to Siberia; many of those living there might have had a different relationship with the space gained only a short while ago; people living in a village may not have lived next to each other for generations, but brought there from elsewhere; their relationships to each other, to their tools and to the animals around them would not have been "traditional" in any manner. This list can go on: the people who had been so terrorized—what did they think about researchers who came to collect their stories and songs? When the interpersonal trust had been so destroyed by surveillance, could the folklorists and the folk freely interact with each other, and did the people apply some form of self-censorship? The crux of what I am trying to say is that the folklorists were collecting traditional folklore in untraditional ways and among folk in untraditional situations.

This complicated situation is multilayered, particularly in terms of communication between the participating actors. Folklorists and folk are only two of those actors; there are the state authorities, the Communist Party, and publishing agencies involved in the initiation and completion of the process of expeditions. Everyone I talked to, in Estonia, Latvia, and Lithuania told me about the ways authors looked for relevant sentences in Lenin's works and literally "inserted" them in their introduction/preface to the volume of folklore they wanted to publish. This insertion was the key to succeeding in publishing the work as well as avoiding suspicion. The act of insertion was a false act, a pretense. It was a compulsion, as nobody seemed to have related with those words, let alone believed in them. Būgienė said, "I was a pioneer at school, learnt Russian really well, did all the right things, but those words, that propaganda never touched me." She narrated an experience she had as a twelve-year-old while listening to Brezhnev on television speaking at the big meeting of Communist Party activists gathered in Moscow from across the Soviet Union: "I felt as if either that was not real or I was not real . . . Even as a child when I could not understand my feelings . . . it was clearly a feeling of being stuck in the molten glass . . . I don't know how else to express it."

I visited several villages in Estonia with Reet Russmann of the Ethnology Department to get a visual reference to the field of Baltic folklorists, particularly in the Soviet period. The most striking signs of the Soviet era are the *kolkhoz* infrastructure: huge buildings for storing grain, for housing the cattle, and for cultural and administrative purposes. The sizes of these buildings cannot but be noticed and mentioned. They bear the stamp of "collectivity." It was collectivity of means of production that required such big buildings. It was the collectivity that required the big buildings for cultural activities. It was the collective administration of collective farms that required big buildings. In comparison with these, the residential areas, all looking the same in every village, were rather small and obviously low quality. Most of them are standing vacant today, boarded up or falling apart and apparently of no use. Even the villages seem largely empty because people are migrating again, "for economic reasons now" as Zirnīte said. After the end of Soviet rule, those who were alive came back to claim their farms, but apparently did not get back to farming. The cultivated farms are today also very huge, but that's because corporate farming has taken over. Corporate farming is also mechanized farming and requires neither many people nor animals. Villages in the Baltic countries cannot return to their pre-Soviet ways of life. Even if the Soviets had not come, ways of life would have transformed and perhaps, like Western Europe, farming would have been mechanized. That would have been transformation, not discontinuity as it is today. Discontinuity creates a vacuum that speaks through signs and symbols like the unused infrastructure of the Soviet period. Those boarded up windows hide realities that no one wants to return to.

As a field of study in the non-Communist world folkloristics has been enriched by several Marxist scholars in the same period. As state ideology in the Baltic countries under Soviet rule, it became the ideology of repression and it is not surprising that no one here wants to visit even the theory of Marxism. The responsibility for this complete loss of faith in the Marxist system of thought rests completely with the state systems as developed by the USSR.

CHAPTER SEVEN

THE RESURGENCE

At the time when the world was too busy watching the fall of the Berlin wall, pondering over the symbolic meaning it had for the end of the cold war and the beginning of a new world order and international celebrations were on at a very high pitch, a serene revolution was taking place in the Baltics. This revolution was so different from any other that hardly anyone took notice of it. It was not using weapons, blaring sound equipment, breaking of any wall, or pulling dictators out of their palaces. Until today, there is little knowledge about it outside of the Baltics.

The Estonians, Latvians, and Lithuanians freed themselves from the oppressive Soviet rule, or occupation, around the same time as the collapse of the Berlin wall and the fall of socialist regimes in Eastern Europe as a result of the policies of the USSR president Mikhail Gorbachev. In the Baltic countries, however, this freedom was gained by singing *songs*: Estonian songs, Latvian songs, Lithuanian songs. Folksongs. The songs about homeland, about home, about the cultural-collective-self: Estonian, Latvian, and Lithuanian selves. The songs that one was not allowed to sing during the Soviet rule. The songs that used to still push their way through in the summer festivals permitted by the state. People who had been pummeled into silence for decades came out of their homes and filled the streets singing together their songs.

Būgienė was part of this moment in Vilnius: "We could feel that we were making history, that we were doing something that kids will read about in school textbooks. Singing, we marched to the television building and took over the broadcast and similarly other institutions." Then the Soviet Union fell. Nobody could believe it, but they seized the moment. And people of the Baltics broke out in songs, a movement that has been called the Singing Revolution. No more the songs of revolution, change and the making of a new society under the Communist Party, but old songs—folk songs—that everyone still knew. Songs of the fatherland, songs of love, songs of nature. Songs that reconnected the people to their habitat and to each other. Songs that established ethnic connection over ideological divide. This was revolutionary and rebellious because they had not been allowed to sing these songs. The Baltic countries became free and established the independent states of Estonia, Latvia, and Lithuania. For years the situation was confused; there was no money, but people were happy.

"A nation who makes its revolution by singing and smiling should be a sublime example to all," wrote the Estonian journalist Heinz Valk, in the June 1988 editorial whose title "Singing Revolution," gave the nonviolent Baltic independence movement its name" (Šmidchens 2014, 3). Guntis Šmidchens's book *The Power of Song* is an ode to this moment of freedom as he writes about the importance of the songs to the Baltic culture and brings together the choral, rock, and folk songs that were sung by millions of people who took their freedom back from the USSR. As the euphoria settled, and they could believe that independence had come to stay and was defined by the membership of the European Union, a new time began.

Baltic Folkloristics since Independence

What happened in the early 1990s, after regaining political independence? Was it a return home or rather an arrival to a previously unknown place? A move from the intellectual centre of the Soviet

West to a less defined position in the European East that came along with the political gains? Like the political changes themselves, which are often perceived as travel and conveyed via the metaphors of spatial movement (cf. "return to Europe"), the transition of scholarly thought from one knowledge regime to another has a lot in common with a geographical experience. When Baltic scholars first re-confronted Western folklore scholarship in 1992, soon after the fall of the Soviet regime, it was almost like discovering a foreign country. (Bula 2017, 45)

Indeed, once the freedom arrived, the journey along a new road started. While the Baltic states had to once again gain their place in the international community of sovereign nations, the scholars had to reconnect with theories and thoughts. For many decades, the scholars and education institutions had remained isolated from Western scholarship, scholars, and institutions. In its inception in the nineteenth century, the Baltic folklore scholarship had not only been a contemporary of intellectual trends in Western and Central Europe but had even pioneered some of its aspects. During the brief period of sovereignty from 1918 to 1938, folklore had been central to the understanding of culture and identity. As we have seen earlier, it was in this period that folklore scholarship was firmly instituted in the universities and institutions like the folklore archives were established in all three countries. The Baltic scholars were in communication with other European scholars, participated in international conferences, and published their works. These connections were particularly strong with Finland and Sweden. It is noteworthy that intellectually it was the Finnish theory and methodology which were the most influential in folkloristics all across the Baltics. During the Soviet period, the centrality of folklore to the cultural politics and policies was displaced and connection with European scholarship severed. Within the Soviet Union, theoretical perceptions were monopolized under the concept of Marxism-Leninism. We have already discussed how these had to govern and define every project and publication.

So, it was after many decades that the Baltic scholars came in contact with the Western world. During these decades, several changes had taken place in the international humanities, which had significantly transformed folkloristics. The three intellectual shifts—one, critique of the combination of nationalism and folkloristics with reference to German romanticism and fascism (Bausinger 1994; Naithani 2014) two, critique of eurocentrism in intellectual perceptions with reference to colonialism (Said 1977), and three, critique of traditional sources for social sciences and humanities with reference to discourse analysis (Foucault)—had transformed the folklore scholarship in the five decades after World War II, the period in which the Baltic scholars had remained isolated from the world outside the USSR. In this context, the theoretical inputs of South Asian and Latin American theorists of "postcolonialism," like Homi Bhabha, Gayatri Spivak, Nestor Garcia Cancilini, and Walter Mignolo had been significant. Another major shift was geographical—the academic world of the United States had emerged as a major center for social sciences and humanities. Within American folkloristics, engagement with contemporary forms of folklore and with performance had emerged as major orientations. While the traditional centers in Western Europe (Finland, Germany) had retained their importance, this new partner was extremely versatile and vibrant in 1990s, drawing its energies also from migrant scholars like Edward Said. Feminism and discourse analysis too had their widest area of influence in American academics. One would think that this geographical shift would have been a completely new factor for the Baltic scholars, but that was not the case. In fact, it was only the fragments of American folkloristics out of all the theories that had had percolated through the sheet of isolation.

Intellectually speaking, the theoretical center had shifted. This shift was not only geographical as major inputs had come from within Western Europe, but it was a shift in perception that had been caused by a combination of factors. Beginning with the Frankfurt School, several theoretical approaches, including structuralism, had been important in changing the perceptions and methods of studying culture. After 1960s feminism or gender theory, post-colonial theory and discourse analysis, formulated and developed by several scholars across the disciplines of social sciences and humanities, had had major influence on the study of folklore. I would, however, argue that around the time the Baltic countries regained their independence, that is at the beginning of the 1990s, the internationally most influential theoretical paradigms were coming from the United states of America. These included the three mentioned above, but specifically in folklore scholarship an emphasis on the contemporary aspects and forms of folklore was the important feature. Challenging the traditional definitions regarding the forms of folklore and pushing the methodological boundaries were distinguishing American folkloristics on its own terms.

The strong influence of American folkloristics visible in current orientations of the folklore discipline in the Baltic countries is therefore a result of the international situation at the time of their independence. Other factors were important too. As Zirnīte said, although the "iron curtain" has been a well-known symbol for the isolation of the Soviet states, "there were holes in the iron curtain," and therefore, information did get through, particularly via the emigres. So, in Latvia, folklorists had been aware of the concern with contemporary folklore in the United States and had read Alan Dundes's *American Folkloristics*. However, full-on contact was new after pulling down the iron curtain. In Estonia, Kristin Kuutma and Ülo Valk told me, the contact with Finnish folklore had existed even during the Soviet period and after independence it was the Finnish scholars who were most keen on connecting up with the Estonian scholars. This contact with Finnish folkloristics also became a connection with American folkloristics, as Finnish scholarship was itself under its influence.

So, with independence came a direct contact with American folkloristics, folklorists, and folklore institutions. Ķencis defined it so: "It was not American folkloristics of 1990s but also of other times, like

Bauman, Briggs, Alan Dundes, Dan Ben Amos, that got introduced. But in 1990s and early 2000s American folkloristics were much more narrow minded and oriented towards practitioners of folklore. In Latvia, it is oriented towards textual studies, archival studies, archival work and looking for some continuities." For other folklore scholars, international folkloristics opened through participation in Folklore Fellows Summer School in Finland in 1994. For Dace Bula, it opened through a scholarship to do PhD research in Sweden. For Guntis Pakalns, it opened through a scholarship to Germany:

> I traveled to Germany for the first time in 1994 after completing my PhD on folklongs. Was invited by Professor Scholz in Münster. I was there for five months, looked at the Zeitschrift for Volkskunde, to find where the folk narrative research departments were, and then wrote down the names of these cities in my travel plan and visited them all: Muenster, Marburg, Goettingen, Freiburg, München, Köln. Brought back a lot of photocopies, looked at courses offered, and attended seminars. So I got a big overview of folkloristics in Germany.

The Baltic scholars were and are faced with a number of issues, and most important among those were the local issues of folklore scholarship and institutions. Nationalism was again important within this local context. Once again, the Baltic peoples had gained independence and the right to express and assert their cultural identity. Issues of language and folklore were important once more and required reclaiming of their institutions and dealing with the changes made by the USSR. The folklore archives, for example, required reorganizing in every possible way. Scholars had to reconnect with folklore scholarship internationally, and they also had to resolve issues of archives, course structures, books, libraries, and so on.

We have already seen in the case of life stories in Estonia and Latvia how the folklorists, ethnologists, and historians quickly got to work recording the folk narratives of a new kind—the life stories of common people. Comparable processes are taking place in Lithuania, too. "More than 20 years have passed since Latvia regained its independence, but increasingly we hear people wondering *who am I?* and *who are we?* Oral history researchers see these questions as being part of a broader issue, namely, how do self-understanding and self-awareness interact and how are they reflected in an individual's narrative about himself/herself?" (Garda Rozenberga 2012, 257–58). This situation of Latvia is to varying extents relevant to other Baltic countries too, and life stories constitute an important subject of study across various disciplines of humanities and social sciences. In Latvia, another recent publication is "Guidelines for Interviewing and Writing of Memories" (Zirnīte and Garda Rozenberga 2014).

The impressive Latvian National Library and the placement of the Folklore Archives in it in Riga speaks volumes about the recognition to the potential of folklore studies. The researchers are busy developing the archives, reevaluating the former manuscript collections, and reaching out to people. Baiba Krogzeme-Mosgorda told me how handwritten manuscripts are being transformed into digital texts so that they can be made available online. This is accomplished by creating a competition among school kids to transcribe from manuscripts, and the one doing the maximum texts in a given time gets a little prize. These transcriptions are then checked by researchers, and an increasing amount of materials are thus being made available through the website.

Since the folklorists involved in the expeditions collected with passion and commitment not dictated by the state, they brought back huge, well-made collections of songs, stories, proverbs, and other folklore materials. Sans quotes from Lenin, the collections in themselves are valuable for now and the future. Analytical work on them can now start. Even older collections has a contemporary value. Already in 1998, the collections of sagas/legends were being used not only by folklore researchers but also by journalists, writers of saga booklets, compilers of historical sagas, ethnologists, archeologists, linguists, theologians, and local historians (Pakalns 1998, 77).

In the Lithuanian Folklore Archives, too, new organization and spirit have taken control. In 2013, the archive hosted the conference of the International Society of Folk Narrative Research and welcomed folklorists from all parts of the world. In 2016, it held the Young Folklorists Conference while I was there. This is a combined effort of the Baltic institutions and brings together PhD candidates and postdoctorate candidates in folklore. Its importance for the future of folkloristics cannot be undermined.

In May 2016, archivists and researchers from the archives in the three countries met in the Estonian Folklore Archives—an occasion I had the chance of witnessing. They discussed the possibility of collaboration. Ülo Valk, as the director of the Institute of Culture Studies and Arts, which includes the Folklore Department was busy giving final touches to an English-language master's program that would run parallel to the master's in comparative folkloristics already offered in Estonian. The English-language program opens this famous old department of folklore studies to international students. The program has recently been publicly announced and began functioning in 2017. This is just a glimpse of what is happening in the Baltic institutions of folklore studies, not a comprehensive list. The amount of research taking place is inspiring but not possible for me to list.

In recent years, the Soviet past and folklore scholarship within that has emerged as a major concern of the scholars in the Baltic countries. This book has drawn heavily from that scholarship as evidenced in the first two chapters. The studies on censorship of the folklore archives, on methods of folklore research within the Soviet period and on theoretical compulsions of Marxism-Leninism have been increasing. The only change that everyone "complained" of was that today research has become dependent on individual *projects,* which, as everybody knows, is about individual scholars being able or unable to get *funding.* The bigger the funding, the more management required, and much research time is lost first in writing the project to get funding and then in managing the accounts. "Along with freedom came capitalism" many said to me. It is indeed welcome, and no one would ever want to return to the nightmare that Soviet rule was, yet the memory of the state funding the expeditions and taking care of all expenses is not a bad one. The question now is: What about the ideologies connected with the Western capitalist world order? The question does not imply only the ideological justification of capitalism as an economic system, but also other ideologies of the Western world: from liberalism to identity politics to post truth. What is the influence of these on the current ideological stance of folkloristics in the Baltic countries? I consider that the current trend of theorizing upon the experience under Soviet rule is a trend that has far more potential than has been expressed until now.

Folklore scholars are reevaluating the history of folkloristics in the Soviet period (Būgienė, Kulasalu, Ķencis). Toms Ķencis is currently studying the so-called Soviet folklore, that is the folklore about Soviet society and leaders that the then authorities were really interested in and the Baltic folklore scholars felt compelled to create. When I met Ķencis in 2017, he was researching the archival materials, and later we conversed about the concept of "Soviet folklore." I reproduce below the transcript of this conversation because what is a drama without dialogue? Ķencis is proposing a new concept, that folklore about Soviet system and leaders collected and created because it was desired by the state is not "fake lore" but authentic folklore.

TK: Now, at the moment, I am finishing an article, unfortunately in Latvian, on Soviet folklore in first Soviet years during the reign of Stalin. And it's the time when something we could call Soviet folklore was collected, not just folklore collected in Soviet time by Soviet folklorists, but very different texts, constructed in very different ways, mediated in different ways than other folklore. And

this folklore of Soviet times one could call Soviet folklore in narrow
term. There were proverbs about collective farming, about Communist Party, and so on.

Me: But those did not exist really so quickly after the occupation by
USSR?

TK: Folklorists I think . . . I should mention that in my mapping article
[referring to his article in the volume *Mapping the History of Folklore
Studies,* 2017] also I write that folklorists were preparing them [peo-
ple] for producing such folklore. Also arriving before time and giving
speeches, also reading the fieldwork notes, asking specific questions
like tell us about 1905 or tell us about Germans, Russians, or whatever
issues, and what's most interesting for me as a researcher that you
cannot call it exactly fake lore like Dorson or as American folklorists would classify it because some Soviet folklorists were asking for
Soviet folklore, but it was real thing; it was just different. It was that
folklore is created on the spot, like the way it is seen today . . .

Me: But it was being created under instructions so how can you call it
real folklore?

TK: Because the definition of folklore includes this creation on the
spot.

Me: That is very true. But this is creation under compulsion . . .

TK: No, I'm not sure that much. They were just generally asking,
please create. . . .

Me: In your last article also, you have shown how these constructions
followed other genre patterns.

TK: Yes. Yes. That's the generic resemblance, and that is what defines
that it is folklore . . .

Me: But then what we understand as folklore is something which is
generally perceived, generally known. If it is not everyone's perception, it is some people's perception at least. I think it's very important what you are saying that it is not fake lore, but I am trying to
understand how it is not fake lore.

TK: Folklore . . . It brings us to the question why some folklore is
authentic and some is not. So, why, why, because no one knows who

created it, but someone created it. It was by one artist. If we just skip this concept of time, then . . . You also said about this society knowing it, but folklore collectors, Soviet folklore collectors ask not just one informant, but many and also explore media, or semimedia, that were participated in, like party committee meetings: Is there some proverb being used, or folklore in wall newspaper, which was popular in the postwar years? There was news about things going on, chronicles about interesting things or events, and it was in the public space, shared. So it was also a source of folklore, Soviet.

The arguments that Ķencis is giving to classify lore about the Soviet systems and leaders, presumably in praise of it, produced in the Baltic countries at a time when the populace in general was living under severe repression, are based on the premises on which the very concept of folklore is created. He questions how we know that earlier folklore was not created on someone's behest. If we understand the "compulsions" behind creation in a broader sense, it is not wrong to say that all creative activity is born of some compulsions, be they social, economic, religious, or political. And yet it is voluntary because a song or a story cannot exactly be forced out of someone, unlike labor, which can be "forced." Another issue, which I hint at in the conversation, is that of people who create and share a lore believe in it. While we have the impression that nobody believed in the Soviet system because people have overthrown it, that is not true because there were people who believed in that system. This belief is recognized in several conversations, including those with Būgienė and Bela. So, why can the lore created under the compulsions of the Soviet system in praise of the Soviet system not be considered folklore?

However, we have also heard about the jokes that were told to mock the Soviet system and leaders. These were neither allowed to be told nor collected. The telling of jokes about the Soviet system or leaders as well as any scholarly interest in them was punishable and could have dire consequences for the tellers or scholars. Aldis

Pūtelis joked about it and said that the biggest collection of these can be found in the archives of the KGB! That sounds true. However, as of now there is no likelihood of anyone getting to study this collection.

Reflecting on the situation of Baltic folklore during the Soviet period, I would say that these two materials—the one collected and is in praise of the system, and the other that mocks that system—together present a brilliant example of the relationship between folklore and power. All folklore is actually divided in these two categories: compositions that praise the powers that are (religious, political, and others) and those that are critical of those powers. In other words, folklore is conformist as well as rebellious. It is for this reason that it has been used by both rightist and leftist forces, has been criticized by some feminists for propagating the patriarchal values, seen as liberatory by other feminist scholars (Zipes 2006; Bacchilega 2013), and presented as evidence of the backwardness of the colonized by colonizers and as evidence of cultural identity by anticolonial freedom fighters (including the Baltic folklorists throughout the twentieth century) (Briggs and Naithani 2012; Naithani 2010; Mignolo 2000; Cancilini 2002). Therefore, one can say that folklore has perhaps always been created under the influence of and in opposition to the powers that be. It contains within itself many ideological orientations, making it impossible to bind all compositions under any one ideology. Above all, folklore is an important character of the drama about the making, unmaking, and remaking of contemporary history and cultural identity.

CONCLUSION

The history of folkloristics in the Baltic countries is evidence of the complex nature of the relationship between power, culture, and the study of culture. By no means are the lines of entanglement straight. The conclusions that have been drawn about the relationship between nationalism and folklore research on the basis of experiences elsewhere do not hold true in the Baltic context. For example, in the Baltic context, nationalism in early folklore research becomes a way of gaining and defining cultural identity so as to be able to emerge from centuries of rule by "foreigners"; the same nationalism makes the study of folklore a form of resistance under the totalitarian Soviet rule, and "folksong" is the banner under which people march to their freedom; and, finally, once they regain their freedom, the resurgence of folkloristics again becomes the way to understand, conceptualize, and represent the lives of common citizens and a symbol of cultural identity in a globalized world order. "Nationalism" in folklore research need not always lead to ethnocentric and violent forms of cultural assertion.

The example of folkloristics in the Baltic countries shows that the study of folklore supports the struggle of people against domination and oppression. As such, the academic study continues to remain in tandem with the nature of folklore as "lore of the folk," as expressions that reflect the lives of the people. The most complex example of this is the Soviet period as it was a state that governed in the name of the people, of the ordinary people, of the working class, and the peasants. Its insistence on folklore as lore that reflects the struggles of the economically stressed populace went to such extremes that it became absurd. The lives of the ordinary people are not made up of only struggles, and a denial of the joys and pleasures of their lives, as also of their spiritual quests, is actually *anti-people*, and that is what the Soviet rule in Estonia, Latvia, and Lithuania became—antipeople. It is not out of context here to refer to the slogan of the citizens of the German Democratic Republic, an independent country in the socialist block dominated by the USSR. At the time of the fall of their socialist state, people marched to the slogan "Wir sind das Volk / We are the People." This slogan truly reflected the tragedy of what socialism had become in the USSR: that people had to remind the state who the people are and what they want. Until that moment, the late 1980s, when the USSR started to be deconstructed everywhere, including the Baltic countries, people had been living under a totalitarian state for decades. During this period of state repression, the study of folklore continued in the Baltic countries, funded by the state and the state power subverted by the folklorists. That "thin layer of rhetoric" (Bula conversation) that the folklorists adopted to cover their subversion was effective in hiding their true commitment to the culture of their land. With the wisdom of hindsight, it can be said that the resistance to state repression by folklorists through the study of folklore in the Baltic countries was successful. I define its success not by the political freedom that was gained by their countries as that was also part of many other processes. I define its success by the fact that almost three decades later, the results of the folklore studies in the Soviet period are considered relevant, useful, and valuable.

This success was also due to the fact that the study of folklore had deep roots, and the methods of study, collection, and archiving had been evolving since the late nineteenth century. The intervention by the socialist state interrupted this process, but for a short period—in its early phase. As soon as a new equilibrium was gained, the process continued, partially open, partially hidden. Therefore, at the end of the Soviet period, the individuals and institutions were quick to pick up the threads and establish connections with their interrupted past once again. We have seen this in the way archives become active again and the way analytical study is expanding and growing. The Department of Estonian and Comparative Folklore in the University of Tartu is emerging as the biggest and the most vibrant department of folklore in Europe. Through this resurgence in the archives and the university departments is emerging an analytical representation of the Soviet period, bringing to the fore aspects of folklore and folkloristics yet unknown to the international scholarship.

REFERENCES AND CONVERSATIONS

REFERENCES

Bacchilega, Cristina. 2013. *Fairy Tales Transformed? Twenty First Century Adaptations and the Politics of Wonder.* Detroit: Wayne State University Press.

Briggs, Charles L., and Sadhana Naithani. 2012. *Coloniality of Folklore. Towards Multiple Genealogies.* Studies in History. Journal of Centre for Historical Studies, JNU. Delhi: Sage Publications.

Būgienė, Lina. 2017. "Lithuanian Folkloristics during the Late Soviet and Post-Soviet Periods: Changes and Challenges." In *Mapping the History of Folklore Studies: Centers, Borderlands and Shared Spaces,* edited by Dace Bula and Sandis Laime, 29–42. Newcastle upon Tyne: Cambridge Scholars.

Bula, Dace, ed. 2017. *Latvian Folkloristics in the Interwar Period.* Folklore Fellows Communication 313, Suomalainen Tiedeakatemia: Academia Scientiarum Fennica, Helsinki.

Bula, Dace, and Sandis Laime, eds. 2017. *Mapping the History of Folklore Studies: Centers, Borderlands and Shared Spaces.* Newcastle upon Tyne: Cambridge Scholars.

Daija, Pauls. 2017. *Literary History and Popular Enlightenment in Latvian Culture.* Newcastle upon Tyne: Cambridge Scholars.

Davoliute, Violetta, and Tomas Balkelis, eds. 2012. *Maps of Memory: Trauma, Identity and Exile in Deportation Memoirs from the Baltic States.* Vilnius: Institute of Lithuanian Literature and Folklore.

Jaago, Tiiu, 2002. *Popular History in the View of Folkloristics: From the Question "True or False" to the Question "What Kind of Truth."* https://lepo.it.da. ut.ee/~lehti/Oralhistory/3.9.Tiiu.htm.

Jaago, Tiiu, Ene Kõresaar, and Aigi Rahi-Tamm. 2006. "Oral History and Life Stories as a Research Area in Estonian History, Folkloristics and Ethnology." *ELORE* 13-1 (2006): 1–15. http://cc.joensuu.fi/~loristi/1_06/jkr1_06.pdf.

Järv, Risto. 2013. "Estonian Folklore Archives." *Oral Tradition* 28, no. 2: 291–98.

Jõesalu, Kirsti. 2017. *Dynamics and Tensions of Remembrance in Post-Soviet Estonia: Late Socialism in the Making.* Tartu: University of Tartu Press.

Kasekamp, Andre. 2010. *A History of the Baltic States*. Hampshire: Palgrave Macmillan.

Ķencis, Toms. 2012. *A Disciplinary History of Latvian Mythology*. Tartu: University of Tartu Press.

Ķencis, Toms. 2017. "The Soviet Project of New Folklore" In *Latvian Folkloristics in the Interwar Period*, edited by Dace Bula, 154–69. Folklore Fellows Communication 313, Suomalainen Tiedeakatemia: Academia Scientiarum Fennica, Helsinki.

Kirss, Tiina, Ene Koresaar and Marju Lauristin, eds. 2004. *She Who Remembers, Survives: Interpreting Estonian Women's Post-Soviet Life Stories*. Tartu: Tartu University Press.

Kõresaar, Ene, and Kirsti Jõesalu. 2006. "Post-Soviet Memories and 'Memory Shifts' in Estonia." *Oral History* (Autumn 2006): 47–58.

Kulasalu, Kaisa. 2013. "Immoral Obscenity: Censorship of Folklore Manuscript Collections in Late Stalinist Estonia." *Journal of Ethnology and Folkloristics 7*, no. 1: 65–81.

Kulasalu, Kaisa. 2017. "From the Estonian Folklore Archives to the Folklore Department of the State Literary Museum: Sovietisation of Folkloristics in Late Stalinist Estonia." In *Mapping the History of Folklore Studies: Centers, Borderlands and Shared Spaces*, edited by Dace Bula and Sandis Laime, 132–53. Newcastle upon Tyne: Cambridge Scholars.

Kuutma, Kristin. 2006. *Collaborative Representations: Interpreting the Creation of a Sámi Ethnography and a Seto Epic*. Helsinki: FF Communications No. 289.

Kuutma, Kristin, and Tiiu Jaago, eds. 2005. *Studies in Estonian Folkloristics and Ethnology: A Reader and Reflexive History*. Tartu: Tartu University Press.

Loorits, Oskar. 2005. "Some Notes on the Repertoire of the Estonian Folk-Tale." In *Studies in Estonian Folkloristics and Ethnology: A Reader and Reflexive History*, edited by Kristin Kuutma, and Tiiu Jaago, 217–42. Tartu: Tartu University Press. Pages

Mignolo, Walter D. 2000. *Local Histories/Global Designs. Coloniality, Subaltern Knowledges and Border Thinking*. Princeton, New Jersey: Princeton University Press.

Naithani, Sadhana. 2010. *The Story Time of the British Empire. Colonial and Postcolonial Folkloristics*. Jackson: University Press of Mississippi.

Naithani, Sadhana. 2014. *Folklore Theory in Postwar Germany*. Jackson: University Press of Mississippi.

Pakalns, Guntis. 1998. "Ein Lettischer Sagenkatalog—Vergangenheit oder Zukunft?" In *The Present-Day Importance of Oral Traditions*, ed. Walther

Heissig and Rudiger Schott, 75–86. Nordrhein Westfallen: Westdeutscher Verlag.

Rozenberga, Ieva Garda, ed. 2012. DZĪVESSTĀSTS UN PAŠAPAZŅA. Mutvardu vesture Latvija. Riga: FSI.

Rozenberga, Ieva Garda, and Māra Zirnīte, eds. 2011. *Oral History: Migration and Local Identities.* National Oral History, Institute of Philosophy and Sociology, University of Latvia.

Skultans, Vieda, ed. *Belonging and Separation in Roma, Russian and Latvian Life Stories.* Riga.

Šmidchens, Guntis. 2014. *The Power of Song: Nonviolent National Culture in the Baltic Singing Revolution.* Seattle and London: University of Washington Press.

Treija, Rita. 2017. "Anna Bērzkalne." In *Latvian Folkloristics in the Interwar Period,* Dace Bula 153–61. Folklore Fellows Communication 313, Suomalainen Tiedeak-atemia: Academia Scientiarum Fennica, Helsinki.

Valk, Ülo, and Tarmo Kulmar. 2015. "Estonian Study of Religion: A Historical Outline of the Twentieth Century Developments." In *Studying Religions with the Iron Curtain Closed and Opened. The Academic Study of Religion in Eastern Europe,* ed. Tomäš Bubik and Henryk Hoffmann. Leiden, Boston: Brill.

Västrik, Ergo-Hart. 2005. "Ooskar Loorįts: Byzantine Cultural Reactions and Prac-tical Application of Folklore Archives." In *Studies in Estonian Folkloristics and Ethnology: A Reader and Reflexive History,* edited by Kristin Kuutma and Tiiu Jaago, 203–16. Tartu: Tartu University Press.

Yurchak, Alexei. 2006. *Everything Was Forever, until It Was No More.* Princeton University Press.

Zipes, Jack. 2006. *Why Fairy Tales Stick. The Evolution and Relevance of a Genre.* New York, London: Routledge Taylor and Francis Group.

Zirnīte, Māra. 2005. Regional Identity from the Perspective of Oral History. Riga: Acta Baltico-Slavica, Archeologia Historia Ethnografia Et Linguarum Scientia.

Zirnīte, Māra, and Ivea Garda Rozenberga, eds. 2014. *Mutvārdu vesturē un dzīvesstāsti. Vadtīnijas intērvetājiem un atmiņu rakstūtājiem.* Riga: University of Latvia.

CONVERSATIONS

Baiba Bela: associate professor and senior researcher at the Faculty of Social Sciences Department of Sociology and Advanced Political and Social Research Institute, University of Latvia, Riga. May 30, 2017, Riga, Latvia.

Dr. Lina Būgienė: senior researcher and vice-director of the Institute of Lithuanian Literature and Folklore, Vilnius. June 1, 2016, Vilnius, Lithuania.

Dr. Dace Bula: senior researcher, Archives of Latvian Folklore and director of the Institute of Latvian Folklore, University of Latvia, Riga. May 29 and May 30, 2017, Riga, Latvia

Vita Džekčioriūtė-Medeišienė: PhD scholar at the Institute of Lithuanian Literature and Folklore, Vilnius. May 19, 2017, Tartu, Estonia.

Dr. Ieva Garda-Rozenberga: researcher, Archives of Latvian Folklore. Former researcher at the Latvian National Oral History Archives, Riga. May 30, 2017, Riga, Latvia.

Dr. Tiiu Jaago: associate professor of Estonian folklore, Department of Ethnology, Institute of Cultural Studies and Arts, University of Tartu, Tartu. June 14, 2016, Tartu, Estonia.

Dr. Risto Järv: head of the Estonian Folklore Archives, Tartu, and adjunct professor, Department of Estonian and Comparative Folklore, University of Tartu, Tartu. June 12 and June 30, 2016, Tartu, Estonia.

Dr. Toms Ķencis: researcher, Archives of Latvian Folklore, Institute of Literature, Folklore and Arts, University of Latvia, Riga. May 29 and May 30, 2017, Riga, Latvia.

Dr. Baiba Krogzeme-Mosgorda: senior researcher, Archives of Latvian Folklore, Institute of Literature, Folklore and Arts, University of Latvia, Riga. May 29 and May 30, 2017, Riga, Latvia.

Professor Kristin Kuutma: Department of Ethnology, Institute of Cultural Studies and Arts, University of Tartu, Tartu. June 9, 2017, Tartu, Estonia.

Dr. Lina Leparskienė: researcher at the Institute of Lithuanian Literature and Folklore, Vilnius. June 4, 2016, Vilnius, Lithuania.

Dr. Margaret Lyngdoh: senior researcher, Department of Estonian and Comparative Folklore, University of Tartu, Tartu. June 9, 2017, Tartu, Estonia.

Dr. Merili Metsvahi: senior research fellow, Department of Estonian and Comparative Folklore, University of Tartu, Tartu. June 29, 2016, Tartu, Estonia.

Dr. Guntis Pakalns: researcher, Archives of Latvian Folklore, Institute of Literature, Folklore and Arts, University of Latvia, Riga. May 29 and May 30, 2017, Riga, Latvia.

Aldis Pūtelis: research assistant, Archives of Latvian Folklore, Institute of Literature, Folklore and Arts, University of Latvia, Riga.

Dr. Aigi Rahi-Tamm: associate professor, Department of Archival Studies, University of Tartu, Tartu. July 4 and July 7, 2016, Tartu, Estonia.

Babu Ram: PhD scholar, Department of Estonian and Comparative Folklore, University of Tartu, Tartu. June 9, 2017, Tartu, Estonia.

Dr. Beatrise Reidzāne: senior researcher, Archives of Latvian Folklore, Institute of Literature, Folklore and Arts, University of Latvia, Riga. May 29 and May 30, 2017, Riga, Latvia.

Dr. Elo-Hanna Seljamaa: lecturer and senior research fellow, Department of Estonian and Comparative Folklore, University of Tartu, Tartu. June 29, 2016, Tartu, Estonia.

Asta Skujyte: PhD scholar at the Institute of Lithuanian Literature and Folklore, Vilnius.

Dr. Rita Treija: head and senior researcher, Archives of Latvian Folklore, Institute of Literature, Folklore and Arts, University of Latvia, Riga. May 29 and May 30, 2017, Riga, Latvia.

Edmunds Šūpulis: researcher at the Institute of Philosophy and Sociology, University of Latvia, Riga. May 30, 2017, Riga, Latvia.

Professor Ülo Valk: head of the Department of Estonian and Comparative Folklore and Institute of Cultural Studies and Arts, University of Tartu, Tartu. June 9, 2017, Tartu, Estonia.

Dr. Māra Vīksna: senior researcher and archivist, Archives of Latvian Folklore, Institute of Literature, Folklore and Arts, University of Latvia, Riga. May 29 and May 30, 2017, Riga, Latvia.

Māra Zirnīte: researcher at the Institute of Philosophy and Sociology, University of Latvia, Riga.

INDEX

Aino, life story of, 65–66, 84
American folkloristics, 92; influence of, 93
American folklorists, contact with Baltic countries, 93–94
Amos, Dan Ben, 94
Andreyev, Andrey Andreyevich, and Finnish method, 30
Anmist, August, arrest of, 26
Archives of Latvian Folklore, 30, 43, 44, 51; establishment of, 20, 21
Atlantic Charter, 23
Atmoda, experience of, 76

Bacchilega, Cristina, 100
Balkelis, 60
Baltic countries, 16–17; freedom of, 3–5; German occupation of, 3; historical changes in, 3; history of folkloristics in, 101; Russian military presence in, 3, 83
Baltic folkloristics: as dramatic, 3, 10; history of, 3–12; after independence, 90–91
Baltic languages, 7; and cultural expression, 16
Baltic scholars, 94; and European scholars, 91–92
Balts, 33
Barons, Krišjānis, 21
Balys, Jonas, 22

Basanavičius, Jonas, 22
Bauman, 93
Bausinger, 92
Bela, Baiba, 77, 80, 81
Berlin Wall, fall of, 89
Bērziņš, Ludis, 28
Berzkaline, Anna, 29, 30, 31; and Latvian folklore, 29
Bhabha, Homi, 92
Bible, translation of, 16
Birkerts, Gunnar, 50
Brezhnev, 87
Briggs, Charles L., 94, 100
Būgienė, Lina, 22, 51, 53, 54, 55, 60, 61, 62, 82, 84, 87, 89, 97, 99
Bula, Dace, 21, 28, 45, 47, 48, 91, 94, 99, 102

Calvinist ideology, 15
Cancilini, Nestor Garcia, 92, 100
capitalism, 97
Catholic Teutonic Order, diminishing of, 15
censorship/censoring: in archives, 39, 56, 93, 96; of manuscripts, 26–28
Christianity, 15
Churchill, Winston, 24
class consciousness, 31
classical folklore genres, 48
cold war, 89

colonialism, 92

Communist Party, 45, 72; cultural policy of, 51; supervision by, 48–49

Communists, 70–71

conversations, in research methodology, 8

corporate farming, 88

Courland, 15

culture/cultural: history, 20, 48; identity, 40–41, 91

Daugava River, 44, 50

Declaration of United Nations, 24

deportation, to Siberia, 39, 52, 53, 55, 60–64, 67, 73, 84

Derrida, Jacques, 27

discourse analysis, 92, 93

Dorpat, 15

Dorson, 30

Dundes, Alan, 93, 94

education, promotion of, 16

Eisen, Mathias Johann, 26

Elmine: life story of, 71–75; Order of Lenin, awarded to, 74

English language, 7

entente powers, 14

Estonia, 3, 4, 36; establishment of, 90; independence of, 13, 73; Kolkhoz system in, 83; Nazi Germany in, 71, 72; Siberian experience in, 64–76; Tsarist Russian rule in, 71

Estonian archives, experience of, 56

Estonian Cultural Archive, 63

Estonian experience, 35–56

Estonian Folklore Archives, 13, 17, 19, 25; censorship practice in, 26–27, 28; manuscripts in, 24–25; Soviet control of, 24–25

Estonian folkloristics, 18, 19, 85; research in, 23

"Estonian Identity," 37

Estonian language, 18

Estonian Literature and Folklore Archives, 76

Estonian National Museum, 43; manuscripts in, 24–25

Ethnic and Narrative Diversity, Latvia, 78

"ethno-cultural sub-culture," 52

eurocentrism, 92

European scholarship, 91, 92

family history, narratives of, 63

fascism, 17, 92

feminism, 92, 93

feudalism, abolition of, 16

Finland, connections with Baltic states, 91

Finnish folklore, 93

Finnish Literature Archives, Helsinki, 18

"folk," 5; folkloristics and, 6, 10, 86–87; narratives, 85; spiritual heritage, 29; traditions, 29

folk singers, appearance of, 52

"folk songs," 89–90, 91; in Latvian studies, 46

folklore: collection, 19, 49, 55; constitution of, 31–33; expeditions, 44, 49, 51 history and, 59, 85–88; performers, 44; research, 4, 22, 32, 44, 52, 56, 85–86; scholarship, 10, 60, 92–94; studies, 3, 5, 35, 40, 93, 102; texts, 53

Foucault, Michel, 92

Frankfurt School, 92

funds, for research in folk studies, 96–97

German language, 7
German Romanticism, 92
Germany, occupation of Baltic coun-
    tries, 3, 13–15, 79
glass mountain, in folktales, 50, 51
Gorbachev, Mikhail, 89
Gorky, Maxim, 31

Helmes, 67
Hinrikus, Rutt, 85
history, and folklore, 85–88
Hurt, Jakob, 7, 18–19, 20, 26, 43, 86

Ieva, 81
Indian languages, 17
Institute of Lithuanian Language and
    Literatures, 43, 51
International Society of Folk Narra-
    tive Research, 96

Jaago, Tiiu, 18, 19, 36, 37, 38, 39, 41, 62,
    64
Järv, Risto, 25, 54, 56, 64
Jaunlatvieši (Young Latvians) move-
    ment, 21
Jõesalu, Kirsti, 82
jokes, at archives, 49–50, 54
Jurjāns, Andrej S., 21

Kasekamp, Andre, 14, 15, 24, 37, 39,
    40
Ķencis, Toms, 30, 31, 32, 33, 45, 93, 97,
    99
KGB, surveillance by, 5, 65, 66
Kirss, Tiina, 65
kolkhoz (collective farm), 31, 48, 67, 72,
    73, 81–83, 86, 87
Komsomol organization, 61–62
Kõresaar, Ene, 65, 76, 82

Krogzeme-Mosgorda, Baiba, 45, 47,
    48, 51, 95
Kulasalu, Kaisa, 25, 26, 27, 31, 32, 33, 97
Kulmar, Tarmo, 46
Kuutma, Kristin, 36, 64, 83, 93

labor camps, 31
Latvia, 3, 4, 20; division after World
    War II, 77–78; establishment of,
    90; ethnic backgrounds in, 78; folk
    stories in, 95; life under Soviet rule
    in, 76–82; in pre-Soviet times, 81
Latvian archives, experience of, 44–51
Latvian folk legends, and tales, 21, 50
Latvian folk music, 21
Latvian Folklore Archives, 32, 43
Latvian National Library, 95
Latvian National Oral History
    Archives, Riga, 77
Latvian scholars, strategies of, 30
Laugaste, Eduard, 36, 37, 38
Lauristin, Marju, 65
Leelo, life story of, 68–69
Lenin, Vladimir, 48, 49, 50; works of, 87
Lerhis-Puškaitis, Ansis, 21
life stories, of deportees, 63, 64, 76–82,
    85
Lina, 83
Lithuania, 3, 4, 83; case before Paris
    Peace Conference, 14; establish-
    ment of, 90; folklore as movement
    in, 21–22; resistance movement in,
    51; under Polish rule, 16; research
    in folklore, 21–22
Lithuanian Folklore Archives, 96; col-
    lection at, 49; experience of, 51–56
literacy, spread of, 15
Livonian community, in Latvia, 17
Livonian song types, 17

Livs, ethnic group, German subjugation of, 15
Löhmus, 27
Loorits, Oskar, 7, 13, 14, 15, 16, 17, 19–20, 21, 22, 27, 56

Magiste, Julius, 38
Mann, Siliina, life story of, 67, 69–70
Marx, Karl, 48
Marxism: and folklore, 6; loss of faith in, 6, 88
Marxism-Leninism, 30, 32, 45, 96; concept of, 91; in universities, 35–36
memory studies, 18, 19, 63
Mignolo, Walter, 92, 100
Milts, Augusts, 77
Minna, life story of, 70–71
"My Homeland," 64
"My Landscape," 64
"mythology," study of, 45–47

Naithani, Sadhana, 100
national consciousness, in Baltic states, 16, 17, 21, 55
"national cultures," 43, 45
National Library, Riga, 43, 44, 50, 77
"nationalism," 17, 51, 94; and folklore research, 101
Naumann, Hans, 30
Nazi Germany forces, in Baltics, 23, 71, 72

Oktoberreita, 61
oppression, in Baltics, 39
Oral History Archives, 78–80
orientation, forced, 31
Osel-Wilk, 15

Pakalns, Guntis, 45, 47, 94, 96
"parallel knowledge," system, 36, 37, 55

Paris Peace Conference, 14
Pavlova, Elena, 25
Pioneers Organization, 61
Poldmae, Rudolf, arrest of, 26
political history, 5
political prisoner, 66
proletarian folklore, 52
Propp, Vladimir, and formalism, 30
Protestant ideologies, 15
Pūtelis, Aldis, 45, 47, 50, 99–100

Rahi-Tamm, Aigi, 64, 83, 84, 85
Ramonaitė, Aine, 52
Reidzāne, Beatrise, 45, 46, 47, 49
repression, by state, 30, 47, 48, 55, 56, 59–60, 62, 88, 102
research, in folklore, 44, 85
resistance, 59–87
resurgence, 89–100
revolution, in the Baltics, 89
Riga, 15, 44; glory of, 50
Roosevelt, Franklin D., 24
Rozenberga, Ieva Garda, 76, 77, 95
Russia, and occupation of Baltic countries, 3, 4, 22
Russian civil war, 14
Russian Communist Party, purges of, 30
Russian culture, 37
Russian language, imposition of, 36
Russmann, Reet, 87

Said, Edward, 92
Sauka, Donatas, 52
Scholz, Professor, 94
Seliukaitė, Irena, 52
Seto singers, folklore of, 33
Siberia: in Baltic history, 60–65; deportation to, 39, 60–63, 73

Siberian experience, in Estonia, 64–76
Singing Revolution, 90
Šmidchens, Guntis, 90
socialism, 31
socialist regimes: in Baltics, 6, 102; fall
    of in Eastern Europe, 89
Society of Regional Studies, 52, 53
Sokolov, and sociology, 30
Solstice festivities, in Baltic countries,
    46–47
songs, in the Baltics, 15, 51
South Asia, 17
"Soviet Folklore," concept of,
    97–98
Soviet period, 4–5, 24, 37, 60–61, 89;
    downfall of, 55, 88, 90, 91; folklore
    in, 22, 40; in historical perspective,
    64, 82–85, 97, 99; life in Latvia
    during, 76–82
Soviet rule, 61
Soviet Union: concept of Marxism-
    Leninism in, 91; fall of, 90
Spivak, Gayatri, 92
Stalin, Joseph, 24, 31, 32, 37, 45, 50–51,
    67; death of, 33; and Soviet folklore,
    33; and USSR forces, 35
Straubergs, Kārlis, 21, 22, 28
structuralism, 38, 92
Šūpulis, Edmunds, 77, 78, 79, 80
Švābe, Arveds, 28
Sweden, and Baltic states, 91
Swedish dominance, 16

Tallinn (torture camps), 67
Tampere, Hervert, arrest of, 26
Tapa militia, 84
thunder god, study on, 47
traditions, struggle against, 31–32
Treija, Rita, 29, 30, 45
Tsarist Empire, regime, 16, 53

United States, academic world of, 92
University of Tartu, 8, 15, 16, 40, 69, 103
USSR, 24, 56, 57, 82, 88; collapse of 3,
    63, 69, 74; minorities in, 71

Valk, Heinz, 90
Valk, Ülo, 46, 93, 96
Västrik, Ergo-Hart, 15, 17
Vėlius, Norbertas, 52
Versailles Treaty, 14
Vīksna, Māra, 36, 40, 45, 46, 47, 49, 50
Vilnius city, 16
Vilnius University, 53, 89

Western folklore scholarship, 91
women, deportee life of, 64, 66–67;
    hard labor for, 65

Young Folklorists Conference, Lithu-
    ania, 96

Zipes, Jack, 100
Zirnīte, Māra, 77, 78, 81, 88, 93, 95